W9-AMU-818

PENGUIN
STUDIO

Canadian
Garden Design
Ideas and inspirations
for your garden

Mark Cullen

PENGUIN
STUDIO

A PENGUIN STUDIO BOOK

Published by the Penguin Group

Penguin Books Canada Ltd, 10 Alcorn Avenue, Toronto, Ontario, Canada M4V 3B2

Penguin Books Ltd, 27 Wrights Lane, London W8 5TZ, England

Penguin Putnam Inc., 375 Hudson Street, New York, New York 10014, U.S.A.

Penguin Books Australia Ltd, Ringwood, Victoria, Australia

Penguin Books (NZ) Ltd, cnr Rosedale and Airborne Roads, Albany, Auckland 1310, New Zealand

Penguin Books Ltd, Registered Offices: Harmondsworth, Middlesex, England

First published 1999

10 9 8 7 6 5 4 3 2 1

Copyright © Mary Mark Communications Inc., 1999
Illustrations © Jack McMaster, 1999
Photographs © Greg Holman, 1999

All rights reserved. Without limiting the rights under copyright reserved above, no part of this publication may be reproduced, stored in or introduced into a retrieval system, or transmitted in any form or by any means (electronic, mechanical, photocopying, recording or otherwise), without the prior written permission of both the copyright owner and the above publisher of this book.

Printed and bound in Singapore on acid free paper.

Canadian Cataloguing in Publication Data

Cullen, Mark, 1956-
   Canadian garden design: Ideas and inspirations for your garden

ISBN 0-670-87639-9

1. Gardens - Canada - Design. 2. Landscape gardening - Canada. I. Title.

SB473.C84 1999   712'.6'0971   C98-930910-X

Visit Penguin Canada's web site at **www.penguin.ca**

Produced for Penguin by Pronk&Associates,
1127 Leslie Street, Don Mills, Ontario M3C 2J6

To Len and Connie Cullen,
my parents, with love

Acknowledgements

Canadian Garden Design has come into being as the result of a team effort, and I am so thrilled with the results that I want to say thank you to some special people.

I am indebted to the folks at Penguin Books (especially Meg Masters) for their inspiration and commitment from the first day I approached them with the idea of creating a book on one of my favourite topics, garden design.

To Weall and Cullen clients and the many friends who provided us with access to their yards and gardens, thanks for your generosity—typical, in my experience, of so many Canadian gardeners.

To Wendy Boyle and Jeff Scott, two talented and generous landscape designers from the Weall and Cullen Garden Centre team, thanks for your inspired contributions and suggestions.

To Wendy Thomas, my co-writer, and Lorraine Johnson, my editor, thanks for making copy flow and words mix in such a way that every English-speaking Canadian can now feel the confidence they need to tackle a garden design project of their own.

Speaking of inspiration and creativity, special thanks to photographer Greg Holman, who possesses exceptional talent in his field. Thanks to the gorgeous photographs in Canadian Garden Design, *I know that many people will be inspired in their own gardens.*

My friends at Pronk&Associates, who "put the pieces together," are wizards—they could put Humpty back together again if they were required to do so. Credit for the reader-friendly appearance of this book belongs to them.

To my dad, for introducing me to the wonderful and creative world of garden design while I was in my teens and twenties: this book reflects a part of you.

To Mary, my wife, thanks for the second opinions and encouragement to launch into another gardening project. I can not imagine a more understanding partner.

And thanks kids! All four of you. You put up with a lot from your dad. I hope one day each of you will understand and share in the joy gardening brings to me.

Contents

Preface

Early on in my horticultural career, when I was nineteen years old, the most wonderful thing happened to me: I was invited into the professional lives of some of the best ornamental plant growers in the business. My dad drove me around Ontario and later British Columbia in the summer of 1975 to all the plant suppliers he was dealing with at the time, through his retail nursery business in Toronto, Weall and Cullen Nurseries. For quite a few summers after that it was my responsibility to seek out the best plant material from the most reliable suppliers and to nurture many of the supplier relationships. Many of these relationships had been created before my dad's time by the late John Weall in the thirties and forties.

At first blush, my introduction was anything but exciting — travelling as we did for miles to view rows and rows of plants in fields and containers. At the time, it didn't seem such a big deal. But meeting these farmers of flowers, shrubs, trees, and evergreens has had a profound effect on my life. Through them came a passion for gardening and a respect for the land and the plants it produces that changed my view of gardening altogether.

The greatest privilege of all was to be invited to the table for a meal during one of these visits. It was always hearty, always generous, often outdoors in the privacy of their own residential gardens and always buoyed by wonderful conversation. There, in their own private gardens, each of the growers described and exclaimed over their visions of a beautiful garden, based on their expertise, experience, and creative approach to the subject.

I will always associate a gorgeous rose garden with the name Bakker, in St. Catharines; the best geraniums in the business with the Shenck family, now in their fourth generation in Canada; Japanese maples with Nick and Paul Reimer of Yarrow, British Columbia; fruit and shade trees, hardy holly and magnolias with John Mathies of Chilliwack; the finest evergreen hybrid boxwood varieties — many of them sought out by enthusiasts in the United States and Europe — with the Stensons of Sheridan Nurseries in Ontario.

My early impressions of these people and their families will be with me forever, as will many of the wonderful things they said. It was after one of these memorable meals, while visiting the Intvens of Connondale Nurseries in St. Thomas, Ontario, that Bill Intven said to me, "Reading is the most sophisticated form of listening. There is no better way to learn." From his experience and wisdom comes the inspiration for this book. Today Bill walks with a cane and I see him only at our annual Landscape Ontario convention. But his passion for plants remains — evident in that youthful sparkle in his eye.

This book is dedicated to Bill and to all the people in the Canadian gardening business who opened the eyes of a young guy in the seventies and eighties. These people are wealthy — and share their wealth. Their interpretation of the word wealth has little to do with money and everything to do with having everything you ever dreamed of, right in your own backyard.

This book is also dedicated to my dad, Len Cullen, for opening the gardening gate and guiding me through. Alice never had anything on this — for those of us who know the magic and balance that gardening can create in one's life, our wonderland is at home.

Introduction

To most Canadians the picture we conjure up in our mind's eye of the Shangri-La of backyard gardens seems completely out of reach. Not true.

I have been to Shangri-La, Canadian-style, and I have seen examples of the Garden of Eden too. I know that they are attainable. They exist in the yards of many so-called ordinary Canadians. I have visited places that can only be interpreted as perfect for the gardener who gardens there. The perfect place for just about anything.

These perfect places always reflect the character of their creators. This is what they have in common, but not much more.

The book is designed to give you a start in creating the perfect outdoor space in your yard — or balcony or deck, for that matter. It is full of photographs and illustrations that need very little explanation and chapters that explain all you need to know to begin. As well, there are sample garden plans, in Chapter 7, which will provide you with lots of inspiration and many practical ideas.

Experienced gardeners have learned that creating a beautiful landscape is not something you achieve and leave. Your garden is always changing, and so are the demands it puts on you in your effort to enhance it.

I might add that the joys you derive from the garden are also ever-changing. Many joys you will not anticipate — which is why more of us are drawn to the magic of the garden every year.

Prepare to be surprised by your garden experience. And ensure that the surprises are good ones by spending some time with this book and putting into a plan the perfect outdoor space — the perfect garden — you imagine for yourself in your own private yard.

Yours, as ever,
Mark Cullen

The Plan and Design

I've heard gardeners say, "Oh, I can't be bothered with a plan. I want my garden to be natural-looking." Many of these same gardeners are puzzled when their gardens don't live up to the dreams they've carried in their hearts and minds.

Claim Your Garden

If you have a passion for cooking, painting, sculpture, or just about any creative endeavour, you can relate to what I am about to say. *Your garden belongs to you.* As time passes, it will become more yours relative to the effort you invest and the benefits you derive from it.

Designing your own garden, or coaching a professional through the process, is an adventure, and your first inclination will likely be to seek help and guidance as you put your plans together in your mind, on paper or in a computer (I will get to that later). But in time you will go your own way; armed with the knowledge and experience of others, you will slowly apply your own thumbprint to your garden and yard.

Consider me — through the contents of this book — and the advice of experienced others — as your coach. Not to be confused with a college professor, we are not here to lecture but merely to guide — to help you manoeuvre your plan forward, avoiding pitfalls, wasted time, and money. Your coaches will help you to maximize the benefits you desire from your garden and to create a thing of beauty you can call *your own*.

And *that* is the point.

Claim your garden. It belongs to you. Investing, as you will, of yourself, your money, and your time in your garden will generate the magic experienced gardeners know but seldom express. It is a feeling that can best be

Planning your garden, and implementing that plan, is a satisfying part of gardening. Be a bit daring – getting rid of front-yard grass is sometimes a big step — and keep things simple.

described as a combination of ownership, a creative expression that is best shared.

The magic evolves from your eventual understanding that the gardener's control over the final product is limited by forces of nature; our success hinges on our ability to work as partners with Mother Nature.

Claim your garden. Share the experience.

Planning Your Garden

Planning — whether it's for a trip or what you'll have for dinner — is really about making choices. Will your holiday be in Canada or overseas? Backpacking in the mountains or visiting art galleries? The answers to these questions will depend on many factors — the cost, the time available, your own interests, and so on. You may even choose to leave some things to chance. So it is with garden planning.

I've heard gardeners say, "Oh, I can't be bothered with a plan. I want my garden to be natural-looking." Many of these same gardeners are puzzled when their gardens don't live up to the dreams they've carried in their hearts and minds. Planning and designing a garden don't mean you have to stifle your creativity — in fact, marshalling your thoughts and assessing your situation will help you make your dream garden a reality.

Curved lines are pleasing to the eye. The installation of this simple path adds contrast of line and texture and beckons the visitor on to see what's around the corner.

Even if your planning is as basic as walking around your yard and marking out beds and paths, you can still benefit from understanding the principles that underlie good design. Soon you'll find yourself looking critically at gardens that "work" and ones that don't. You'll understand how a certain effect was achieved and why it's pleasing to look at. Don't be embarrassed to stand in front of an interesting garden making notes — and if the owner is working there, so much the better. You can pick up some new ideas from chatting with someone who's solved some of the problems you face. This type of sharing and learning goes on all the time with gardeners. As you study gardens, you'll recognize that some very pleasing effects are the result of breaking the "rules."

In the pages that follow, I'll give you ideas you can apply to your garden so that you can have a beautiful garden with as little — or as much — work as you want. One of the things I love about gardening is that it slows me down. Spending just a few minutes every day in the gardening season doing what I call "serious puttering" takes the tension out of my shoulders and lets me catch my breath. I also like being able to appreciate the beauty of my garden without feeling that it's a big responsibility.

For most of us, gardening is a way to relax, to unwind, to connect with the natural world. Each of us, as we think about the garden we want, takes personal needs and desires into account. Some people want a nice-looking garden to maintain the standards set by neighbours but don't want to spend a lot of time on upkeep. Others love collecting a variety of plants and want a garden that shows the collection off to its best advantage. Others want to include play

areas for children in their gardens. Sometimes, these various interests are all fighting
for attention in the same garden, and it can
be hard to decide which will take priority.
By working through a series of questions,
you can begin to sort out what's most
important to you.

*Planning small spaces is as important as
planning for larger areas. A lovely little corner
like this will come under more intense scrutiny
than a larger space.*

Is it necessary to have a plan? Yes, you need a plan if you want to save money and time by planting the right plant in the right place the first time. It may exist in your head or on a few scraps of paper, but if you're a beginner, I'd strongly recommend you have a plan that's worked out on paper. On pages 16 and 17 I've laid out some ideas for getting started with pencil and paper. This plan, like your garden, will probably end up as a work-in-progress as you refine and change it, but it will always be a good reminder of your original vision if you start to feel you're losing your way.

No matter what your level of experience, or whether you're facing a new garden or renovating an older one, a plan will help you focus your thoughts and force you to deal with the realities of your site. Although you're undoubtedly eager to start transforming your yard, it's best to spend a year planning. A year sounds like an incredibly long time, but over the months you'll observe how the changing seasons affect your garden. For example, you'll discover how the sun's daily and annual movement changes the play of light and shadow in your garden, where the prevailing wind comes from, which parts of the garden are exposed to rainfall, and which are protected. You'll need time to observe your garden from every window of your house at all seasons and times of day. If you're working with an existing garden, you can still give your green thumb exercise by keeping your plants pruned and watered and the beds weeded, and by growing lots of annuals to liven up your yard. Those who are dealing with a brand-new yard — usually a carpet of green grass — can liven it up with some

If you don't want to spend a year observing the garden, hire a landscaper or landscape student to do an analysis of the garden, especially noting sun and shade.

container plants. Moving them around with your garden furniture will enable you to see your garden in different ways.

I've found it takes about three years to absorb the details of and become familiar with the natural surroundings of your home and to know what you want your finished landscape to look like. If you're planning a renovation, you probably already know this. I suggest you implement your plan over at least two years — after you've spent a year developing it.

The garden designers at Weall and Cullen, our garden centre operation in Ontario, have found that our clients often don't want to be presented with a plan for their entire property but prefer to work on a particular section of the garden each year. These sensible gardeners know that a job is less daunting if it's broken down into its parts. Although you may start by sketching in ideas for the various sections of your garden — the front yard, the backyard, the side yard — in the beginning concentrate on the part that's most important to you. If that's the backyard, usually the largest area to be worked with, break that down further into its components as well. Each year you'll see progress, but you won't feel overwhelmed — financially, physically, or emotionally — by undertaking what are really several landscaping projects all at once. As you implement your plan over several seasons, your expertise as a gardener will grow, and you'll find yourself approaching the rest of the plan with more confidence.

The challenge facing any gardener is to bring together your needs and your family's with the constraints of your site to result in the garden of your dreams. Sounds impossible? Not at all! Yes, some compromises may need to be made along the way, but rest assured that you'll discover creative solutions as you go. Start by asking yourself how you'll use the garden. The design adage "Form follows function" applies to garden design, too. It doesn't matter how lovely or unusual your garden looks if you can't use it or live in it. Putting together the design is a balancing act — balancing your needs, the restrictions of your site, and the fantasy garden that exists in your mind. But as any good designer knows, you start with function: how it will be used. As you ask yourself the following questions, be brutally honest. This is not the time to be dreaming — that part comes later.

Assessing Your Needs

In preparing any kind of design, you need to start by asking some fundamental questions. You want your garden to reflect your interests and style; to complement the architecture of your house; and to incorporate as

Assess your garden in different seasons. This flowerbed will look very different in mid-summer, not only because of the different plants growing, but because of light conditions.

As in a house, different functions — housekeeping and play areas, for example — overlap in the garden. Planning for how they will work together is part of the fun of design.

unobtrusively as possible the "housekeeping" aspects of gardening — the placement of hoses, compost bins, garden sheds, and so forth.

The garden expresses to others who you are, not only by what you plant in it but by what you do in it. It's easy to overlook the everyday things the garden is already used for — a playground, a dog run, an outdoor eating area — and it can be hard to imagine other ways the garden could be used. Put yourself in the role of landscape designer and "interview" yourself. Use the following questions to help you consider all the things you would like in your dream garden, ranking the items according to their immediate importance to you. Some items might end up on a "nice-to-have-someday" list. For example, you may be busy with a young

family, so low maintenance is important to you right now, but as the children grow up, you'd like to spend more time gardening. For now, put those plans for a labour-intensive rose garden on the back burner — but you can sketch in the spot where it will go ten years from now. In the meantime, the future rose garden could make a great spot for a sandbox.

Assess Your Uses

Whether you're designing a garden where none has existed — the situation faced by those who've moved into a brand-new house — or are in the mood to renovate, ask yourself all these questions. It's a worthwhile exercise, for you may see your old garden and its uses with new eyes.

🌿 Who uses the yard? What do they use the garden and yard for?

These are the most important questions you'll answer. Although you may feel confident that you know who uses your yard, spend the next few months consciously taking note of the traffic in the front, back, and side yards. You may be surprised at what you discover about the parts of the yard that are used and how they are used. Do the kids head to the front yard or the backyard to play? Whichever it is, you'll want to make room for a spacious play area there. Where does the dog or cat like to snooze? There's no sense planning to plant some tender perennials in that spot — your dog or cat is likely to think you're just providing a nice soft spot for it to catch forty winks. What about your spouse? Does he or she like to sit on the back steps with a cup of coffee on a warm Saturday morning? Look at the garden from that spot to see how you can incorporate a good view — a charming flowerbed, perhaps, or a spectacular individual plant such as a magnolia, or a whimsical piece of topiary.

Just as important is to ask who doesn't use the yard. Perhaps the non-users genuinely don't like the outdoors, but it may also be the case that access to the garden isn't inviting. By simply changing the way that steps or a path lead into a garden, you can make the garden much more welcoming. Ask your family what they want from a garden. Throw out a few ideas to them to get started — do they want a place to play, a place to entertain visitors, a place that will attract birds? Visions of a mini-Disneyland may have to be nipped in the bud, but involving the family in what the garden will look like will mean that the space will be used by all members of your family.

As you observe your front and backyards, note the routes people use in and around the house. How do visitors enter the house and access the garden? Does the mail carrier jump over a flowerbed? What's the access for meter readers? How do you bring the groceries in from the car? Will you need space for an extra car someday? These sound like mundane considerations, but they will all affect the way you design your garden. Now is the time to start thinking about how to incorporate practical matters with beauty, even though some parts of your plan may not be implemented for a few years.

Then there's the dream garden that exists in your imagination. What do you imagine yourself doing in it? Are you playing with your children? Working in the flowerbeds? Sitting in a wicker chair with a cold drink and a book? Cooking at the barbecue? Your vision may not reflect the reality of your life, but it should influence the practical considerations you're making. Your wish list is not only for the garden you need today, but also for the one you desire in ten years' time, even in twenty years' time.

🗩 How will you enter and move about in your garden? Will there be paths and gates?

When you were observing how people used the yard, you noticed how they entered the garden. You may have found that there were natural entrances people used to get into the yard, access routes as varied as through a hole in the hedge, down a muddy path, or across an existing flowerbed. However hard you try, you may find it impossible to break those habits. Rather than frustrating yourself, work with what you've got. The muddy path is easily fixed — interlocking brick or flagstone is not difficult to install and can transform a problem route to an attractive feature. If the dog or kids like the hole-in-the-hedge entry, you could prune the entry to make it a bit larger and more formal, with an arbour, for example. Tidying it up will make it look as if it was always meant to be used as a doorway to the yard. Ask yourself why the route across the flowerbed is preferred. Is there no other easy way to get into the yard? Is it a handy shortcut? If you can provide a better entry, you may be able to save your flowerbed. However, if it becomes clear that the path across the flowerbed is the most natural one, a few stepping stones, firmly installed to give good footing, will at least keep wayward feet on the path.

Right now, you're less concerned with the materials the paths and gates will be made of and more concerned with where they go and what they do. In Chapter 4, I'll talk more about gates and paths, not only about the different materials and their upkeep but also about the effect they can create.

And where do other paths lead? Is there a purpose to them, a logic to the route they encourage? Do they beckon and entice the visitor to go farther? These questions apply to paths that you're planning to install. You have a wonderful opportunity to introduce an air of mystery by combining a path with a gateway, or designing a path that curves gently, revealing more and more delights as it guides you through the garden.

One of the great challenges for the garden designer is to motivate garden visitors to move their feet — and preferably not in retreat — to explore, to venture out, and discover the mysteries of nature that are a part of every garden.

To help accomplish this, a garden must go somewhere. When all the discussion about themed gardens, use of colour, the addition of furnishings, and so on is over,

garden design must above all provide adequate temptation to avoid the guest's taking one look from a convenient vantage point, exclaiming how attractive everything looks, then seeking out the nearest chair to discuss the weather, politics, religion, education, or something similarly less signficant than gardening!

For a garden to go somewhere, it must never (well, almost never) dead-end. A visual dead-end is an invitation for rejection of footsteps. And surely one object of the successful garden is to share it with others. My answer to this is to keep in mind that each garden "room" should provide a path or gate or steps that go somewhere.

A lovely carpet of grass is more than a delight to the eye — it's a great cushion when little ones take a tumble.

If gates already exist, ask yourself what purpose they serve. Are they utilitarian, meant to keep animals out or in? Are they there for security? If they are rarely closed, why bother keeping them? Can a decorative gate be installed to match the style of your garden and the architecture of your house?

🍃 Do you have pets that need a place to run?

A dog can be the most difficult pet to accommodate in a garden, especially in a small one. Fencing off an area for the dog is the usual solution to protecting planting areas and lawns. A chain-link fence can be a decided eyesore, but consider masking it with a hedge, a bed of tall perennials, or a

mass of morning glories or other twining vines. Provide some shade for the dog to shelter from the direct sun in the summer.

Cats — your own or the neighbours' — frequently claim a napping spot in a flowerbed or under a shrub. Over time, that area gets worn down and the plants just give up. Much as we love our four-footed friends, we may not want them turning our flowerbeds into bedrooms. Make a note to remind yourself of this when you get to designing the flowerbeds — you can try to

Defining space is part of designing a garden. Here the plantings are for passersby to admire and help delineate the public space and the more private space near the house.

thwart cats with a low hedge of a plant such as lavender. Its branches are just prickly enough to discourage a cat.

🍃 Do you want to add free-standing structural features such as a gazebo, arbour, or pergola in the garden or incorporate a deck, verandah, solarium, or porch into your house? Do you want a greenhouse? Where will you place benches and other seating in the garden?

Now is the time to dream. If you plan now on adding a special feature several years in the future, you can set that spot aside for now — plant some annuals or short-life perennials or use it for the kids' playground until you're ready to start building.

Structures such as gazebos, arbours, and pergolas can give a romantic and at the same time practical touch to a garden. Gazebos can be used for a variety of purposes: a place for an afternoon cup of tea, a rainy-day play area for kids, or simply as a trellis over which clematis or climbing roses can drape themselves. If the gazebo is a place for sitting, try to situate it so that there's an attractive view, preferably a surprising one that's not visible from other parts of the garden. Decks, verandahs, solariums, and porches extend the enjoyment of the garden and make a visual and physical link between the house and yard. They're great for decorating with plant containers; you can sit on covered decks, verandahs, and porches on rainy days; and a solarium lets you enjoy the view of the garden all year. I'll talk about these structures later on, but for now just decide if you want them on your wish list.

A greenhouse is the dream of every avid gardener, but they're not always the most attractive feature of a garden. They should be situated to take advantage of the sun, but once you've accommodated that requirement in your plan, look at ways you can make the surrounding area more attractive. A low hedge of roses separating the greenhouse from the rest of the garden, for example, will draw attention away from the greenhouse. If you've been gardening a few years, you'll know whether you're likely to use a greenhouse. If you're a beginner, I'd suggest waiting for a while — you could set aside a spot now for future use. In a few years' time, if you decide a greenhouse isn't a good idea, use the spot for some other garden structure.

Even a small garden has room to tuck away a small bench or two. I like to see a bench at the end of the garden, both to look at and to sit on. There's something peaceful about it, away from the hurly-burly of the household activity, and it gives the gardener a chance to view the garden and house from a different angle. A bench situated near a scented plant invites the visitor — or the weary gardener — to sit and "smell the roses." Although a stand-alone bench or chair is the most usual type of seating, an old tree stump or a big rock can be called into service as a place to sit. I'll give some hints about what to look for in garden furniture later in the book, in Chapter 4.

And while you're thinking about these structures and seating, how about a treehouse for the kids — or even for you?

🍃 What are your parking requirements?

If you don't already have a garage or parking pad, this is the ideal time to contemplate adding it. If you're going to install front-yard parking, check out your local bylaws to see what the requirements are. In

addition, you'll need to make sure there's enough room for car doors to open comfortably and for people to get in and out. The rule of thumb for driveways is a width of 3.5 m (12 feet); a parking area should be at least 2.7 m (9 feet) wide and 5.5 m (18 feet) long.

🍃 Do you like to eat or entertain outdoors? If so, how many people do you need to accommodate?

Whether it's barbecuing or elegant alfresco dining, there's nothing like eating outdoors, but cooking and eating outdoors in comfort requires a large "floor" area. Table and chairs need to be set on a sturdy surface such as a wood deck or brick patio. People should be able to move around easily without worrying about knocking over chairs, damaging plants growing on the deck or patio, or even falling off the deck. If you have trouble visualizing how much space you'll need, set out the table and chairs, or

Don't forget the views from indoors! No matter the season or weather, this is the view of the garden you'll have more frequently than any other.

experiment using indoor furniture to see what makes you feel comfortable.

Plan for a place to keep the barbecue and equipment such as extra gas containers. You'll want to keep it close to the kitchen but not too close to windows, either yours or the neighbours'. The position of a gas barbecue might be dictated by the source of the gas supply; check this out while you're drawing up your plans.

You'll need to protect cooking and eating areas from sun, wind, and rain, so incorporate awnings, trellises, lathing, or umbrellas into your plan.

🍃 Will a swimming pool or hot tub be part of your garden?

Look into your crystal ball and see if there's a swimming pool or spa in your future. Families with kids over the age of five are most likely to get lots of use out of a home swimming pool. Situate it close to the house so you or another adult can keep an eye on the water activities. Check out municipal bylaws — municipalities often have specific regulations regarding safety issues, such as child-proof fencing around the pool. Even if your kids are water savvy, your neighbours' kids may not be. Regardless of bylaws, a child-proof fence around your pool — *inside* your already fenced yard — is a good idea.

You'll need to provide a weatherproof shelter for the pump and filtration system. You could combine those structures with a changing room and an outdoor shower area. For now, don't plant the area with expensive or large-growing trees and shrubs. Sketch in where the electricity for the pool or hot tub will go. It's better to get it roughed in now than to have to do extensive renovations to install it later. You'll find more information about these features in Chapter 4.

No matter where you keep your gasoline-powered mower, be sure there's good ventilation in case of a fuel spill.

🖏 Where will you keep your tools and equipment? Where will the garden hose be positioned?

When you've invested good money in a special spade or pair of clippers, you expect to get many years of service from it. The best way of ensuring that is to have a special place for your tools and equipment. It doesn't have to be large but should be dry and secure. Part of a potting shed could be used as a toolshed. If you plan to store a lawnmower in the shed, ensure the door is large enough to accommodate it and that there aren't any steps that make getting the mower in and out a backbreaking job. Of course, if you prefer, you can use the basement to store many of your gardening equipment and use the extra outdoor space for more plants!

The source of the water supply often dictates the placement of the hose, so if it looks as if the hose will be an eyesore, you could design a little housing for it or plan to screen the area with lattice or a shrub. Whatever method you choose to make the hose less conspicuous, ease of access is paramount. I especially like a hose reel — it saves a lot of frustration. The hose doesn't end up snaking all over the garden to be tripped over, as it's easy to wheel it where you need it.

🖏 Do you want to install a watering system?

This is the time to do it! If you're interested in low-maintenance gardening, an automatic underground watering system can cut down on the time you spend watering (you don't want to cut down on enjoying your garden!). Take the time now to look into the various watering systems — some of them very sophisticated — and lay the groundwork now for the one you choose. The range available increases all the time — you can get sophisticated systems with timers and flow regulators.

🖏 Do you want to incorporate lighting features into your garden?

Strategically placed lighting can enhance your garden, increase the amount of time you spend outdoors enjoying it, and add to the security of your home. To help work

Drawing Your Garden Plans

Here's a project to make the winter fly by! Challenge yourself to come up with two or three designs for your garden, keeping in mind your wants and needs. Just for the fun of it, design a formal garden, if that's what you hanker after, even if it's not practical right now. Now how does a cottage garden look in the space? In the end, you may use elements from these fancies in your final plan.

Play with colour, shape, height, texture. Use the ruler to draw the straight edges of property lines and buildings, then put it away. Just relax — draw free-flowing shapes and experiment with colour.

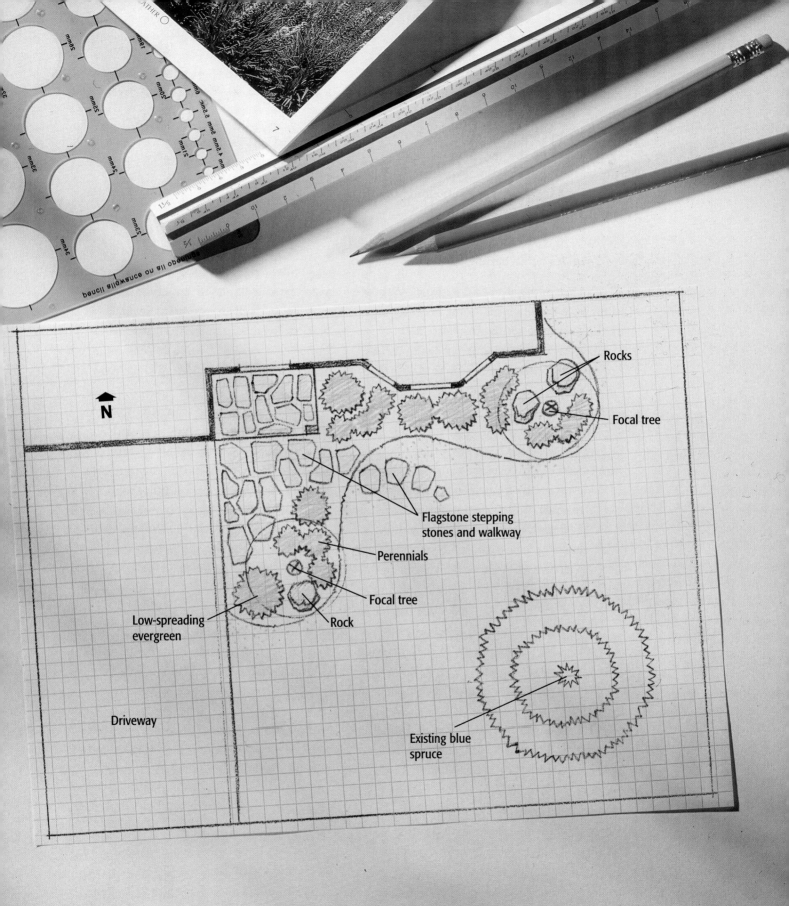

N

Rocks

Focal tree

Flagstone stepping
stones and walkway

Perennials

Focal tree

Low-spreading
evergreen

Rock

Driveway

Existing blue
spruce

lighting into your plan, talk to an outdoor-light specialist to see what's involved and learn about safety requirements. Without advance planning, trying to incorporate electricity into the garden in a few years' time can be a frustrating experience. See Chapter 4 for more details about lighting systems.

🍃 Do you want to compost? Have you got room for a rain barrel?

I can't imagine gardening without composting. It's incredibly satisfying, not only because you're cutting down on the garbage at your curbside, but the finished product — nutrient-rich compost — is the *best* thing you can possibly add to your garden.

A composter doesn't have to be an unsightly addition to your garden. Many commercial composters, available at nurseries or at a reduced price from many municipalities, are unobtrusive and even fairly attractive. If you build your own, you can build it to suit the space available to you in an out-of-the-way corner of the garden. Don't make it too out of the way, though.

You need to be able to get to it easily, summer and winter. A good place is outside the door nearest the kitchen — that's where a lot of the raw material for the compost comes from.

The old-fashioned rain barrel is making a comeback, I'm glad to report. Not only are the new ones just as good at water conservation as the old ones, but the new ones have some improvements, too. They're often made of recycled plastic and have a built-in screen to keep insects and debris

Put some compost in a cloth bag and hang it in a rain barrel. Water your plants with this nutrient-packed compost tea.

out. A spigot at the bottom will give easy access to the water in the barrel.

🍃 Is privacy important to you? Will there be parts visible from the street as well as private parts to your garden?

The garden usually presents two faces: the public, which is often at the front of the house, and the private, at the back. The public part can represent the values and interests of the neighbourhood: it might be a safe place for kids to play, a smooth green carpet of grass, or even an exuberant vegetable garden. Even though the front yard is the public area, clever planting can camouflage an area to make it private and sheltered from the public gaze.

A uniform feeling is achieved by repeating themes in the front and back yards, whether it's a theme of colour, texture, or style. However, this is not always possible to implement because of the varying needs of family members. Many gardeners dream of a private, secluded garden, where they can get away from things, relax and enjoy the peace, but if you also need to accommodate a kids' play area, you may think you have to forget the idea for a few years. With a bit of ingenuity, though, you can probably carve out a little corner with a comfortable chair that gives you your magic spot.

🍃 Do you want a place for a clothesline?

Although most Canadian homes have gas or electric clothes dryers, there's nothing like the smell of clothes dried in the sun — and you're saving energy too. My wife, Mary, judges a "good" day by whether it's a "good drying day."

You don't need a big space to make a small clothes-hanging area. If you've got a

bit of space in an out-of-the-way spot, perhaps along the side of the house, and it just doesn't seem to be good for anything else, make this your "outdoor laundry" area. A wooden table nearby is useful for holding the clothes basket and clothespins. On nice days, you can use it to fold the dry laundry. Ideally, you don't want to look out into your clothesline but you don't want it too far from the house, so it's an easy dash to bring

There's often beauty in simple and unexpected compositions. Some things you can't plan for — it's called serendipity — and such things are often fleeting.

in the clothes in a flash storm. The umbrella type of clothes dryer has the advantage of not taking up too much space and could easily be situated behind a lattice "wall." Smother the lattice with morning glories or clematis and hanging your clothes up will be an enjoyable experience.

Assessing Gardening Styles

Let's move into a different set of questions now. These have more to do with the horticultural aspects of the garden — what you like to grow, what you want to grow. We're still talking about function because these questions consider what you want your garden to do.

🍃 How much time do you want to spend gardening?

Be honest! There's a difference between "want to spend" and "ability to spend." As I mentioned earlier, I enjoy puttering in my garden, but not everyone has the time or inclination to spend hours weeding, deadheading, watering, and so forth. You can keep these chores to the minimum and still have an attractive and pleasing garden. Cutting down on mowing and watering by getting rid of grass and installing drought-tolerant plants; choosing low-maintenance materials for paths, fences, and gates; and preventing weeds by mulching will result in low-maintenance beautiful gardens, leaving you more time to enjoy the other things you want to do. Most perennials are low maintenance, needing deadheading occasionally and dividing every few years. Annuals can be a bit demanding, since they need deadheading to keep them at their best. Plants in containers are fairly high maintenance, as they need watering daily, often more frequently in windy weather.

You might find you've got a discrepancy between "want to" and "ability to," so check out the description of the low-mainte-nance garden in the chapter on Garden Styles.

🍃 Is a lawn important to you?

The advantages and disadvantages of lawns is one of the most hotly debated gardening issues these days. I can't imagine my garden without a beautiful green carpet. The lawn is like a welcome mat, not just to be walked on but also to welcome the eye — a cooling introduction to something beautiful. Others believe that lawns are high maintenance, what with mowing, watering, fertilizing, weeding, dethatching, and raking. But when it comes to design, what does a lawn do? A well-cared-for lawn will show off your plants to perfection and tie the various elements together. The smooth green can offer rest to the eye, as well as provide a canvas for light and shade to play on. A lawn can calm a garden in a way no other ground cover can match as it offers an antidote to bright colours and bold foliage. From a more practical point of view, grass makes a good surface for kids to play on — you may not want to spend the time and effort to produce a picture-book-perfect lawn, but a layer of spongy grass will prevent many a scraped knee.

A lawn is inexpensive to install, especially if you start from seed, so it makes a satisfactory short-term solution to covering an area, even if you want to replace it in the future. You'll find that the lawn will bear foot traffic better than any other ground cover. As well, I think a lawn, produced from top-quality grass seed and sown on well-prepared ground, is the most attractive ground cover — anywhere.

🍃 What style of garden do you want?

This question, closely related to the next question, refers not only to low-maintenance or specialty gardens such as meadow or cottage gardens but what might be called the theme. Later in the book I describe some of the traditional styles — formal Italian, for instance — that are still used as the basis for many gardens around the world. Many of these styles are not practical for today's gardeners, but you can incorporate modified versions into yours. Keep in mind, though, that good garden design accommodates itself to the architecture of the house, so your style may be one that's appropriate for the lifestyle of a Canadian in the late twentieth century — a nice display of plants, some lawn, and an area for relaxing and playing in.

🍃 What style is your house?

When I travel across the country, I love to see how architecture varies from region to region. I'm not talking about differences as profound as that between an Italian villa and an English country cottage. The differences are more subtle, and a visitor to our country may not be aware of them, but I'm convinced I would be able to tell that this

Even the vegetable garden provides visual delights. Consider growing vegetables among the flowers and shrubs. Be a bit daring!

stone farmhouse would be found in the Quebec countryside and that wooden one is probably from Vancouver Island or the lower B.C. mainland. The architecture of your house is a vital element of your landscaping plans and each should complement the other. A white picket fence around a sophisticated downtown house is as out of place as an ornate wrought-iron one around a cottagey bungalow.

Consider, too, the era your house style evokes, especially if your house is more than fifty years old. Luckily, most Canadian houses lend themselves to a wide variety of designs, whether it's a romantic white garden or a stylized Japanese garden. In fact, the furnishings — the little extras such as fencing, walls, gates, paths, garden ornaments — lend as much, if not more, character and style to your garden as your choice of plants.

While you're pondering your house, look for little architectural features and recurring shapes and lines. Echoing these shapes and lines in your plans will give the end result an air of professionalism. Peaks and curves in roofs and around windows and doors can be duplicated in the shape of flowerbeds and the design of steps, gates, and fences.

🍃 Do you want to grow vegetables or herbs?

Vegetables and herbs don't need a lot of space, but they need sun to be successful. Vegetable gardens cannot be considered low maintenance. Many vegetables, such as carrots, zucchini, lettuce, beets, beans, and peas, are grown from seed, and this entails preparing the soil, planting the seeds, keeping them watered (and protected from squirrels, dogs, cats, and sometimes even kids), cultivating and weeding, and in some

cases eventually staking. But there's nothing as satisfying as the first peas or beans or tomatoes from your very own garden!

If you have a small area, you can make intensive use of the space by training vegetables such as beans and peas up a trellis. As well, herbs and miniature vegetables are right at home in containers, as are lettuces. Reserve a sunny corner on the deck for these veggies, although lettuce needs to be protected from bright noonday sun. Try a mesclun mix in a container outside the kitchen door for a quick summer salad.

Another good use of space is to intersperse vegetables with flowering plants. Not only do you get the produce, but their foliage often adds interesting textures and contrasts.

A well-maintained lawn: the pride of many Canadian gardeners. If you've got the space, a lawn can provide a cool and calming frame for your garden — and for your home.

🍃 Do you want a specialty garden — water garden, rock garden, rose garden?

The answer to this question will spring from your own likes and your ability to maintain the plantings. I love roses and have created space in a sunny spot in my front yard for sixteen plants. Long ago, I decided the attention they require is worth it. On the other hand, although I like other people's rock gardens, I'm not interested in investing in the maintenance they require to stay looking good.

If you're looking for the easiest roses to care for, try some of the hardy shrub roses.

You may find yourself with a site that cries out for a special kind of garden. A tricky slope presents the gardener with challenges, not the least of which is mowing it. Assess the slope to see if a rock garden can be installed. Rock gardens need good drainage, usually not a problem on a slope. Another advantage of rock gardens is that they don't need to take up a lot of space, and because many rock garden plants are small, you will have the enjoyment of being able to grow a wider variety of plants in this space than in a traditional perennial bed. On the other hand, rock gardens are high maintenance and demand a significant time commitment to keep them weed free, so it's a good idea to start small. Many of the plants suitable for rock gardens are sun lovers, so look for a sunny slope.

Many plants used in water gardens perform best if the pond is situated in a sunny spot, too. If safety is a consideration, you'll need to incorporate fencing in your design. Use the excavated soil to build up your garden or to build a berm — a small rise that can act as a windbreak or a feature to make the garden more intriguing. A water garden doesn't have to take up a lot of room — even a square metre can support plants and a few fish.

Roses need sun, good air movement, and rich soil. They often do best in a bed by themselves, where they can make a stunning and scented display. Most roses don't fall into the low-maintenance category — many need pruning and winter protection and are targets for insects and diseases — but for a lot of people, including me, they're well worth the effort.

🌱 Are you a plant collector?

Some gardeners get interested in one type of plant — for example, the hosta, lily, peony — and when they visit a garden centre, they find themselves attracted to these plants, no matter what other enticements are around. If you're like this, you're a plant collector at heart and you can have some fun with shapes and textures and colour. Even a garden full of hostas can be exciting and lovely, as there is a wide range in size and colour of leaf. A border of hostas on either side of a grass path can usher the visitor into a garden in style. The daylily is another example of a plant that lends itself to collecting. The many varieties available today mean that your garden can be in bloom for most of the season with an assortment of colours and flower shapes.

Most of us fall into the rather broad category of "collector of plants I like the look of." This is the type of collecting that leads to a garden full of variations on the daisy or full of plants with ferny foliage. Somehow, once we get the plants home and in the garden, they lose their distinctive character because they melt into the other daisylike flowers. You need some contrast, but if collecting is the most important thing to you, you can still have a beautifully designed garden by planning your plantings using colour as the unifying theme. Group white plants together, drifting into blues or pinks or yellows. Of course, you'll have to be sure those plants have the same requirements with regard to sun, moisture, and nutrients.

🌱 Do you want to attract birds to your garden?

Birds and gardens go together naturally. In a thoughtfully designed garden, birds can find just about everything they need: food, nesting material, shelter from predators, and water. If you're interested in attracting birds to your garden, get to know the types of birds that frequent your area, and research the plants that can provide them with shelter and food.

Plan places for birdhouses and feeders. Feeders should be situated as far away as possible from fences, trees, shrubs, and any other object a squirrel can launch itself from. When tempted by tasty birdseeds, squirrels can jump amazing distances — a couple of metres, at least. And even quite slippery posts don't seem to deter them.

Birdhouses, also called nesting boxes, should be located at least 1.5 m (5 feet) above the ground. They should be protected from direct sunlight and heavy rain, but you also want to be able to see them from your house or a comfortable viewing spot in the garden. There are different types of birdhouses for different species, so do some research on the types you want to attract.

Birdbaths also attract birds. Set one in fairly protected area — preferably near a shrub in which the birds can take shelter when they feel threatened by a predator such as a cat. A birdbath on a high pedestal can be set in a more open area. As with birdhouses, different kinds of birds have different requirements for how they take their water and bathe in it. Any good book on attracting birds to your garden will provide advice.

Assessing Your Site

Hand in hand with deciding what you want from your garden is the assessment of your site — the geography of your particular bit of Canada. This step is vital to the success of your garden.

Fifteen years ago, there were more than 600 varieties and species of hosta to choose from. Today, there are more than 2,000 and new ones are added every year.

Assessing your site is a year-long undertaking, just as assessing your needs was. Fortunately, you can do them concurrently! Some questions you'll ask yourself about the site can be answered quickly, but accounting for all the factors can take longer.

🦃 What shape is your lot and how does it relate to the position of the house and other buildings?

The shape and size of your lot are two inflexible facts you'll have to deal with. You can't change them, but you can change the effect they have on your garden. A long narrow lot can be made to look wider by dividing the yard into separate areas. Because dark objects appear to be closer and pale objects look to be farther away, you can use colour to create a sense of intimacy or spaciousness. A planting of dark green evergreens at the end of the garden will make the space between the house and evergreens seem smaller than it is. A fence draped by a rambling rose covered in masses of white blossoms will make the distance seem greater. The same principle can be applied to furniture and structures. When you choose colours and paints, be aware that the colours can have a profound effect on how space is perceived.

If you expect to draw a plan to scale, take the dimensions of the garden, ideally in the spring, when it's easier to get to every corner of the garden. You can simply "pace off" your lot — a pace is usually about a metre or a yard — for a rough idea of the size of your lot. But if you intend to draw up a very accurate and detailed plan, you'll have to get out a sturdy tape measure. An up-to-date survey can suffice. Be sure you've got the dimensions of all buildings and structures, including decks, driveways, and positions of large

trees. Don't forget to take note of directions — where north, south, east, and west are. These reference points are the most important of all, as they will help you recall where sunlight falls.

Where does the sun fall? How does it change the way the garden looks from early morning to dusk? Here the sun acts as a spotlight, featuring different plants and combinations as it moves across the sky.

🍃 What are the views from the different parts of the garden? What are the views from different rooms of the house?

If you've ever been stopped dead by a beautiful garden or can't restrain yourself from buying a gardening magazine full of lush photographs, you know the importance of the visual aspect of planning your landscaping. A view may be attractive or you may consider it a blot on the landscape. You want to enhance the former and maintain views that cause delight every time you or a visitor looks at it. For the latter, you need to decide if you can obliterate an unattractive feature or view by physically removing it, hiding it, or drawing the eye away from it. A good view can be framed by plantings, and the eye can be directed to it from several parts of the house and garden. Conversely, a charming piece of garden decoration can deflect the eye from an unsightly view.

No matter where you live in Canada, you're probably forced by weather to spend more time indoors than you'd like. So the views from the house to the garden are important. Looking out over your yard from every window of your house also gives you different — and valuable — perspectives. Viewing your garden from a height, such as a third-floor deck or balcony, can help when it comes time to do a bird's-eye plan of your garden as it helps you relate how things look from above to how they look at your eye level.

🍃 What plantings, landscaping, and structures already exist? Can you work with them?

It's a rare yard that doesn't have something growing in it, so most garden designs are really renovations rather than "from-scratch" creations. If you've already got photographs of your garden at different seasons and over several years, you know that early spring and late summer are very different seasons in the garden. The lush growth of August makes the garden a completely different place than it was in the spring. That's one of the things I like about our Canadian climate — the way the changing seasons almost redesign the garden.

Look at the existing plants with a critical eye. What do you want to keep? If a plant is not earning its keep, consider pitching it out (onto the compost heap, of course). Or plan to move it while it's dormant to a spot where it will flourish. If low-maintenance gardening and a beautiful garden are your twin goals, there's no room for plants that need coddling and still don't quite live up to expectations. Don't be nervous about

Whimsy has a part to play in the garden. It's usually found in the finishing touches but can also be incorporated into the practical gadgets that gardeners love.

moving perennials to a new spot — sometimes it gives them a new lease on life.

More of a problem, though, are the larger plants — trees and shrubs. If you're not satisfied with them, try to figure out what the problem is. Perhaps some judicious pruning will perk them up. Not all plants are worthy of being saved — that may sound hardhearted, but you'll enjoy your garden much more if it looks great and isn't a burden to care for. Before you call in someone to cut down a tree, though, there are two things to do. Check to see if there are any legal restrictions to doing so. But just as important is to see if there is some unpleasant view or feature being hidden by the tree.

If there is, you'll have to factor that in to your design as something to be dealt with.

You may change your mind about getting rid of the tree, but if the tree has to go, you have an exciting opportunity to do something really creative to solve the problem of the disliked view or feature. Depending on the layout of your site, you could install a comfortable sitting area there — even a gazebo — so that you always sit with your back to the unattractive view! But if the view is visible from the house, call on tricks such as installing something so stunning that you're not even aware of the background: a fountain, a piece of sculpture, a pergola. If you decide the tree has to go, it's a nice gesture to warn your neighbours of your plans even though the tree is on your property; in many ways (although not legally), it also belongs to those who view it and perhaps have loved it from afar. They may mourn its passing more than you do.

Existing landscaping and structures may have to be incorporated into your design or earmarked for removal or change in the future. Financial resources can act as a brake on a wholesale overhaul of your garden, and in some ways that can be a blessing. As you implement your plan season by season, you may be glad you didn't put a "scorched-earth" policy into action. Once you've made the first few changes, you may be pleasantly surprised by how the yard has come alive.

🍃 What zone are you in?

This question becomes important when you get down to the details of plant choices. Plants have varying degrees of hardiness. Some will survive extremely harsh conditions; others won't make it through a winter. We all like to push things a bit to see if we can grow something that's not supposed to make it in our particular zone, but for low-maintenance gardening, get to know your zone and the plants that grow there. That way, you won't be replacing plants every year that you hoped would last for a long time. There's more information about zones in my book *The All Seasons Gardener*, with some hints about extending the seasons and protecting sensitive plants.

Spring and fall are the best times to move, divide, or transplant perennials.

🍃 What type of soil is in your garden?

Soil types range from sandy through to clay. In between is that sought-after soil, loam, which is a mix sand, silt, clay, and humus. Sandy soil has a light, loose texture and will fall apart when a handful of it is squeezed. Sandy soil drains quickly and does not hold water. Silt holds its shape when squeezed. Damp clay also holds together when squeezed, but falls apart if it's dry; clay tends not to drain well. Good garden loam holds its shape. However, all "garden-variety" soil needs help, and I'll cover this subject more thoroughly in Chapter 5, where I discuss the final step in design, choosing the plants.

Another aspect of soil that should concern you is the nutrients it contains, as well as whether it's acid or alkaline. To check for acidity or alkalinity, you can buy a testing kit, but a few clues from your surroundings can help you figure it out. Limestone rocks are usually present in areas where the soil is alkaline; granite stones suggest the soil could be acid.

It's harder to ascertain what nutrients are present. You can have your soil assessed by a private testing lab, a university, or your provincial department of agriculture for a fee. If your soil is low in nutrients, you can gradually restore it to health by adding compost or buying a load of soil called triple mix (one-third compost or composted cattle manure, one-third topsoil, and one-third peat moss) and digging it in. Mulching all beds will help improve the soil, as well, but this can be a long process. Don't despair if you find yourself in the predicament of having poor soil — consider making raised

The Camera as a Design Aid

The camera is a great help in preparing to design your garden. Starting in the spring and continuing through summer and fall, photograph your yard — front, back, and sides— from different perspectives and at different times of the day and season. Then spend the winter with those photographs — either get several sets of each snapshot printed or have colour photocopies made. You can mark on them, paste things over them, cut them up, do whatever you want as you play with the garden plan. I find this especially useful if you're one of those people who has trouble visualizing what your plans will look like. A few gardening magazines can provide pictures of benches, gates, plants, and so forth that you can cut out and use. Use a stick of non-permanent glue so you can switch and change colour schemes and arrangements as you move the elements around.

Taking photographs of your garden throughout the year will help you remember where you've planted things, when they come into bloom, what they look like at different times of the year. Start a scrapbook of these photographs to help you to track the progress and history of your garden. If you have a video camera, use that to record your garden — you'll get sound and movement, and it's inspiring to watch it in the winter.

beds as part of your garden design. You'll need to buy soil to fill them, but you won't have the backbreaking work of digging. Compost or leaf mould are also great additions to any soil.

- What is the topography — the lay of the land, in other words — of your site? Are there drainage problems?

The topography of the garden will dictate the design to some extent, especially if the site slopes steeply. The opposite end of the extreme, a perfectly flat site, can be challenging to deal with too. Ideally, you'll be working with a yard that has gradual changes in height since it is visually more interesting, but in small spaces there's usually not

Composting — it doesn't need to take up a lot of room and the results will more than repay you for the space given over to it. Once you've planted flowers and shrubs, you need to keep them healthy, and compost is part of that important task.

enough room to accommodate more than one level. If you have the room, you can construct a berm — a small rise — by mounding up earth, turf, and other discarded material then finishing with a layer of good soil. A berm should look as if it naturally belongs where you situate it, however. Have a look at gardens with berms and see for yourself what looks successful and what doesn't.

Drainage is an important consideration, especially on a site that has poor drainage. Many plants will not survive in poorly drained soil, although there are some lovely bog plants that need to have their roots in damp soil. Wooden structures sitting on damp soil will begin to rot more quickly than if they were on drier ground. As well, locating structures such as storage sheds or benches on damp ground will not make their use appealing.

Soil that has water sitting on it for more than an hour is considered to be poorly drained. If drainage is a severe problem on your site, the wisest course is to consult a landscape designer who is knowledgeable in dealing with these situations. Solutions include building raised beds over the area; raising the height of the bed by adding several inches of soil; digging out the soil to below the planting level and adding a layer of gravel — 6 to 8 inches (15 to 20 cm) — in the bottom of the trench before replacing the soil; digging out the soil, adding gravel as just described, then putting in weeping tiles that drain to a dry well. This last solution is best undertaken by a professional. If poor drainage is only a moderately irritating problem, dig in lots of compost, which will help absorb some of the moisture and improve the drainage capabilities of the soil.

Quick-draining sandy soil can be amended by adding compost over the years, although you can also turn this feature to your advantage: you can plant that section of the garden with plants that prefer dry soil. In some cases, especially in new suburbs, the site has been prepared with correct drainage in mind, and attempting to change it could cause unforeseen problems.

🍃 Where do sunlight and shade fall?

This seemingly simple question is as fundamental as knowing your zone for plant selection. The amount of sun and shade, and the type of shade, will restrict the types of plants you will be able to grow.

Where sun and shade fall will change throughout the year, not only because of trees and shrubs that are in leaf or not, but also because of the position of the sun in the sky at different times of the year. At the risk of repeating myself, this is one important reason to observe your garden in every month of the year before you start drawing up ambitious landscaping plans. Pull out the camera and start photographing your garden. Don't worry if these snapshots aren't works of art — you just want a record of the different parts of your garden at different times of the year so you can remember where that big oak casts its shade in August, or how the shadow cast by your neighbour's garage changes from spring to fall. Especially if you're gardening on a small lot, you want to take advantage of every nook and cranny of growing space. Dealing with the situations you can't change — where buildings are located, high rainfall, long winters, and so forth — can lead to wonderful discoveries of plants that grow in seemingly impossible conditions. Of course, those hard-to-grow-in spots don't necessarily need to be used for plants — you can turn them into a peaceful sitting nook, a dog run, or a mini-basketball court!

Understanding where light and shade fall and how they change throughout the seasons can be used to great advantage to produce a "layered" garden. In a shrubby area of the garden, spring bulbs will flourish before the shrubs leaf out. As the shrubs

The reward of thoughtful planning and planting: a garden that matures gracefully.

come into leaf, shade-loving perennials and annuals can be used to grow through and hide the dying foliage of the bulbs. Suddenly there's a new layer of growth in the garden.

🌿 Which direction does the prevailing wind come from?

Once you've established where the prevailing wind comes from, you can plan to break its force by planting a hedge, or "living screen," if wind is a problem. Knowing the direction of the wind also tells you where the sheltered spots in the garden are. Take advantage of these spots to create a little microclimate. This is an exciting way to garden with plant material you may never have dreamed was suitable to your conditions.

You may find that a natural wind tunnel has been created in the space between two houses or between a house and garage.

Solid walls also cause problems: wind eddies over the top and swirls down the other side, in effect acting like a small whirlwind. The best windbreaks filter or reduce the wind. Once again, handy trellises can come to the rescue and be used for a quick fix. At one end of the "wind tunnel," install a trellis. A more permanent windbreak is provided by evergreens such as spruce, pine, and cedar, which are fast growing.

You've completed the first part of designing or redesigning your garden. As you've seen from the questions you've been pondering, designing a garden is challenging but exciting. It's an interesting mix of the principles of design, horticulture, and construction. Because of the complex interplay of these elements, I'd suggest you read the whole book before you begin to draw up your plans. Even if you thought you didn't have a designer's bone in your body, you'll find you're approaching design with more confidence and knowledge.

2

Approaching Design

You can start to make your dream garden a reality without spending a lot of money or wasting hours of valuable time that could be better spent enjoying your garden.

Up until now, the questions you've been asking and answering have been pretty practical. But garden design is also about a *vision*. To prepare the framework for your garden, it's useful to understand a bit about the principles of design and how to go about implementing those principles. That way, you can start to make your dream garden a reality without spending a lot of money or wasting hours of valuable time that could be better spent enjoying your garden. I'm going to outline the basic principles of design that every landscape designer, architect, interior decorator, and graphic artist learns. There's nothing magic about these easy-to-understand basics. If you're one of those people who seems to have a natural instinct for what is pleasing to the eye, it's worth knowing *why* it's pleasing. On the other hand, if you're someone who just can't seem to get it right — no matter what you see in your mind's eye — study these principles because applying them can fix some of your disappointments.

Balance

Balance is one of the most important and fundamental design concepts. Implemented well, balance will give a garden a feeling of comfort and peace. Our eyes seem to demand balance, so an unbalanced design is unsettling.

Visually, your garden extends beyond the fence. Choose what you want to screen out and what you want to keep in. This tranquil scene offers ideas that can be adapted to many situations.

Symmetrical Balance

Symmetrical balance is an easy concept to explain by looking at a formal garden. In such a garden, there is a central line or axis from which all design elements flow. If the central line is a path, the path's width is evenly bisected by this imaginary central line. An urn placed at the edge of the left side of the path would be balanced by an urn placed in the same spot on the right side. A group of plants on one side would be matched by a group on the opposite side, and they would be matched exactly — golden marigolds with golden marigolds, for example. Everything on one side of the central line is a mirror image of everything on the other side. Such formal layouts are rarely seen in Canadian gardens — they can require quite intensive upkeep, for one thing — but if the architecture of your house is formal and balanced, you may want to carry out the symmetry in the front garden, at least.

Even in an informal garden, there may be a corner that you want to be a bit more formal to give an air of sophisticated elegance. A symmetrical arrangement will help you achieve this: a bench flanked by matching junipers, for example, or a rectangular pool with matching urns at each corner planted with the same type of flowers or foliage.

Asymmetrical Balance

Asymmetrical balance is a bit more complex than symmetrical. The important word to remember is *balance*. Just as a scale can be made to balance when items of varying weights are added in the right combination even though the items differ in size, colour, and texture, so a visual balance can be achieved by using plants, furniture, and decorations to make an equal "weight."

To avoid a lopsided look when you design an asymmetrical setting, pretend that the main elements have a weight. Imagine placing them on a scale. Do they seem to balance? If not, your asymmetrical arrangement isn't truly asymmetrical. For example, a tall pyramidal Japanese yew might be roughly equal to three rounded dwarf Japanese hollies — the volume of the three hollies being equal to the volume of the yew. If you want a more open plant to balance the hollies, you would need more of them because the "visual weight" of each open plant is less than the visual weight of each denser holly. As you observe plant combinations, look for these "visual weights" and you'll soon get the idea. There's no hard-and-fast rule about the relation of these weights, but when you understand the concepts, you'll feel more confident in your ability to make pleasing plant combinations. In addition, you don't always need to achieve balance through size; you can balance a large plant with one that has a bright colour.

The visual weight of the plant is influenced by its leaf density and colour. Dark-leaved plants look heavier than a plant of the same size with lighter leaves. Plants with dense branches and needles, such as a Colorado blue spruce, look heavier than plants with loose needles and more open branches, such as an eastern white pine.

Asymmetrical designs provide creative tension and make an arrangement lively. As mentioned above, introducing a more formal (symmetrical) section —perhaps a small rose garden surrounded by a clipped hedge of boxwood — into an informal

(asymmetrical) design can provide some peace and tranquillity. Don't be intimidated by this talk of "weight" and "volume" — this is not a mathematical equation. The look you achieve will provide satisfaction based on the time and thought you give your plan at these early stages. Think of the process as being similar to decorating a room. Take your time and make thoughtful decisions. And don't be afraid of mistakes — they can always be fixed later.

Harmony and Contrast

I describe harmony as a "pleasing and peaceful look and feel." It does not mean that everything should be the same, which can become boring. It's okay to be attracted to a certain type of plant and incorporate it

A sense of symmetry exists in this informal setting. The trees and shrubs are balanced on each side of the inviting gazebo. There's vertical interest on both sides, complemented by the rounded shape of the evergreens.

into your plan. Some gardeners naturally gravitate to plants with delicate ferny leaves and graceful nodding flowerheads — cosmos, flax, 'Moonbeam' coreopsis; you may like the bold foliage of euphorbia or hosta. But a garden full of similar plants soon becomes tedious.

Surprisingly, contrast can bring about a feeling of harmony. Contrast is achieved when each element has something to offset it — a foil. You can have a lovely display of feathery-leaved flowers, but offset them with the contrasting leaves of the hosta or the rigid blades of the iris's foliage. Match mounding shapes with upright clumps. Colour can be used in the same way — to suddenly introduce a contrast or foil to make the whole picture bright and lively.

When you're looking for plant contrasts to provide harmony, remember that all the plants must need the same growing conditions. Also, the plants should not contrast in every way. For example, dwarf conifers make a nice contrast with mounding heathers because the former are upright and the latter are lower growing. However, their fine leaf structure and colours can be quite similar. They both like similar soil and light. In the shady garden, hostas and ferns make for wonderful contrast. Their form is similar, but the leaf texture is decidedly different. Get to know plants well (colour photos in gardening books or suppliers' catalogues are useful) and decide what their most important characteristic is — weight, shape, texture, or colour. Then use that idea to match or contrast plants with one another.

Group after group of flowering perennials and annuals can be tiring to the eye. Use foliage plants to break up those expanses of colour. Plants with silver foliage and ornamental grasses are especially valuable in the garden, for they mix well with hot or cool colours and make welcome transitions from one colour scheme to another. Taller ornamental grasses add variety to the height and texture in the border.

If you don't want to use plants as contrast, objects such as stones or boulders can be set by a path or at the edge of a planting of similar shrubs. A piece of statuary set among plants of similar habit or colour can offer all the change that's needed.

Scale

Scale refers to the relative size of things, and because it's relative, there's no hard-and-fast way of deciding what can be considered too big or too small in a particular spot. Sometimes we have a niggling feeling there's something wrong, but we just can't put our finger on it. Start to think about scale, and you may suddenly see that the flowerbeds are too big or small in relation to the size of your property and house. Delicate foundation plantings may be lost against the large sweep of brick that's the front of your house. These are problems of scale. Generally, the larger your property, the larger your beds and decorative elements can be.

Most of us want our gardens to look bigger, which can be difficult, not only because of small urban lots, but because we're competing with the ultimate in space — the sky. The sky makes everything under it seem smaller. Add that to suburban housing lots that are too narrow or too shallow, and you've got your work cut out for you! But by manipulating scale, you can fool the eye.

You can make a small area seem larger by breaking it into even smaller sections, each with its own character and main point of interest. Replacing the lawn with winding paths will give the illusion of a larger space, particularly in long, narrow gardens. Manipulate the scale — the length that's too long for the width — by introducing an interruption, such as a fence or specimen plant, especially if it's set on the axis line so that you can't see to the end of the garden. Now that the eye can't see the end, the garden will seem wider. If this is not an option,

Add interest by making even minor changes to paths. A step or two signals a change and gives vitality to a landscape.

place a feature closer to the house so that the eye is drawn to it and not to the end of the garden.

Another aspect of scale is the relation of people to the garden's size. Is there room for them to move about comfortably? Do low-growing branches overwhelm the visitor? A narrow path can be an impediment, or it can be an invitation to investigate the flowers that tumble along its sides. Recall the items that were important to you in the needs assessment and how people will be using the garden.

This tidy composition has pleasing texture, colour, and echoing shapes — the round evergreen, the rounded impression of the blanket of flowers, and the soft edges of the stone.

Repetition and Rhythm

Repeating colours, shapes, or textures can impart a sense of unity to your design. Earlier, when I was discussing the style of house you have, I used the word echo to describe this idea. When you pick up a design element in the architecture or existing landscape and repeat it in the shape of an archway or trellis, a flowerbed, or a

A beautiful focal point for year-round enjoyment. The planting in the urn can be changed to reflect the season. Note how the edge of the paved area is softened by the misty blue foliage.

water garden, you're using the concept of repetition, rhythm, or echoing. You'll create a feeling of relaxation and peacefulness.

Another way of introducing repetition is to plant flowers in drifts — imagine a clump of flowers, then stretch one or both ends out, and taper it off. In your mind, you've just created a drift. In the flowerbed, drifts of flowers can tie colour schemes together or take the eye to a contrasting colour. As you plan the drifts, repeat some of the plants farther down the bed. You'll be amazed at the pleasing effect you've created.

You can also repeat shapes. A boxwood or yew can be clipped into a rounded shape. A gazing globe set nearby repeats the shape. Plants with rounded growth habits — lady's mantle, lavender, and artemisia, all with loosely rounded looks, and pinks, some of which are denser, smaller, and more compact — will have the same effect.

Focal Point

A focal point is anything — a special plant, a structure, a piece of furniture, a statue, a birdbath — that draws your eye and makes you want to get nearer to it. Generally, it is located at the far end of the garden, but a garden, even a small one, can have two non-competing focal points. When you go to the end of the garden and turn to look back, another focal point may have been created that beckons you to return. But too many things competing for attention can be confusing and as a result, there is no focal point. So good old conventional wisdom would have it that one focal point for a small garden is the rule. In larger gardens that have been divided into "rooms," focal points in each room should be visible from the preceding room, tempting you farther into the garden.

Plant material makes a good focal point. An existing tree that has qualities that make it worth keeping is a ready-made focal point. Trees that have a lovely shape, interesting bark and leaves, and are attractive all year long can be the point around which your whole garden revolves.

Focal points can be used to help create optical illusions. A focal point placed on the sight line from the window from which the garden is viewed and at the farthest part of the garden will make the garden seem longer.

Rooms

Many garden designers have found it's beneficial to transfer some indoor decorating approaches to the outdoors. Indoors, the house is usually already divided into rooms, and even open-concept houses have areas designated as places for eating, cooking, bathing, sleeping, entertaining, and so forth.

You can think of your garden and outdoor areas as one big room, or a series of small rooms. Adapt the open-concept plan to divide a large yard into several smaller rooms — a "living room," a play area, a work area, and so on. This technique of picturing rooms can enable you to increase the use you get from your garden. And when you think about it, your property has probably already been divided into at least front and back rooms — your front and back yards. However you choose to divide your garden, be sure that each room has a purpose — to eat in, to display a collection of sculptures, to work in, to grow herbs, or as a quiet place to sit and read — so that the visitor or gardener is tempted to stay — just for another five minutes.

The style of garden you want can be reflected in the way you lay out these rooms. Rooms for a formal garden are often rectangular in shape but can also be round or oval. Fences and hedges are used to clearly define the rooms. The ground is usually level, but if your lot slopes, terracing it would be in keeping with the formal feeling. In an informal design, rooms are less clearly defined, and beds of shrubbery, ground covers, or even berms of earth can mark divisions.

Fences and hedges make great dividers, but even flowerbeds can provide the necessary separation between two parts of the garden. If your yard is small, rooms can be separated by something as unobtrusive as a low boxwood hedge or a rock garden planted to separate two parts. A small garden can appear to be made larger by dividing it in half — a perfect way to apply the "rooms" idea. In all but the very smallest yard, you can usually give over a corner for a small water garden, a sandbox, a herb garden. A comfortable chair can be at home in a shady corner.

Arbours and trellises are dividers that become the "doorways" of different garden rooms. They serve two purposes — as a transition and as an opportunity for growing vines and climbers.

The "hallways" — the narrow side yards or alleys between houses, usually shady spots — can be brightened up with foliage plants with interesting texture, but plants aren't the only solution to the problem of decorating these sometimes lost spaces. Paving material that links front and back will give a feeling of unity. Interesting pieces of sculpture, big or small, or strategically placed rocks and boulders can all enliven an otherwise forgotten area of the garden.

A wonderful example of the ways in which the lines and shapes of the house can be echoed in the shapes used to define the flowerbeds. This planting draws you in!

Another room often forgotten is the equivalent of the mud room or workroom or basement — that place where we store all the things we can't bear to throw out, where we repair household items or store the less attractive items that keep a household going. Outdoors, the equivalent might be the garbage bins, the dog run, the compost area, perhaps even a place for drying clothes. If they're important to you, you want to include them in your design. But you also want to conceal these rather unappealing necessities. The answer lies in concealing and enclosing by using hedges, trellises, and fences. When you're adding these to your design, leave enough room for comfortable access, or such areas will never be used properly. The hedge or trellis will do double duty by not only hiding the offending view, but also as something attractive in itself — a hedge makes a peaceful green background for other plantings or gives the eye a rest from a nearby lively planting. Unless the hedge is densely branched, it would be best to use an evergreen hedge so there's year-round screening.

A trellis can provide support for a flowering vine or one with interesting foliage. Add some variety by using a different fast-growing annual vine every year instead of a perennial covering. Or, if year-round covering is important, use an evergreen vine such as euonymus.

Fences also offer the opportunity to grow vines and climbers, while concealing what lies behind. The fence itself can become a special feature as long as it is successful in completely hiding its secret — the material, the colour, the pattern can all add to the interest of the fence, diverting attention even more successfully from what's behind

A tapestry of foliage — it offers privacy, blocks unsightly views, and is restful to the eye. The variety of colours and different heights give it life.

it. Don't despair if you've inherited or decided you need a chain-link fence. It makes a strong enclosure for a dog or a vegetable garden but also can be clad in a wide variety of twining vines. Alternatively, plant a hedge or row of tall plants in front of it.

The View

Many of us with urban gardens, especially small urban gardens, are surprised at the idea of a view — we might think of a *view* as one of those languid English landscapes. We might think view is a rather grand term for what we see from our kitchen window. But even if you're staring at a neighbour's wall or a clutter of poles and wires, you still have a view — not a nice one, to be sure, but a view nonetheless. If this is what you're facing, think about ways you can obscure it or deflect the eye away from it. Adapt some of the ideas I talked about in hiding the utility

areas. A whimsical piece of folk art can attract attention, as can a stunning specimen plant, such as a lush old rose or an interesting corkscrew hazel.

If you're among the fortunate and have a wonderful view from some part of your garden, decide what you want the view to do for you. Perhaps you want to see the view when you sit out on your patio. Put yourself in that very spot when you start to design the way you'll emphasize or frame the view. Sit on the patio now to be sure that the garage roof hasn't obscured the view. You might want to replace your patio with a raised deck if the view is fabulous! A less disruptive solution might be to install an enticing path to lead the visitor to a better spot from which to see the view.

Thinking Like a Designer

When you sit down with that piece of paper and pencil, you may find yourself brought to a dead stop. Comfort yourself with the thought that it takes landscape designers several years of training to become knowledgeable and proficient. In many cases, they've had to train themselves to think and see like a designer. It's second nature to them now, of course. You don't need all that training to come up with a great plan for your garden. With the ideas and principles I'm outlining in this book, I think you'll start seeing your yard and its possibilities in new, exciting, and creative ways.

In addition to the aspects of designing I've mentioned above, designers are acutely aware of space — where it is, how much there is of it, whether it's being used well, whether it could be used in other ways, how different elements relate to one another. Start to think about the space around you. How do you feel within that space? Enclosed? Hemmed in? Safe? Exposed? By changing the way the space is arranged, you can profoundly change the feeling evoked. This can be hard to imagine, but you can begin to test out how different spaces affect you by going on garden tours and visiting public and private gardens.

A trick some designers use when approaching a landscape design is to imagine that space is not empty but rather is solid. Think of a big block of Styrofoam you're standing inside. Then begin to carve out, from the inside, the shapes that the plants

and other parts of the garden will make. It's an interesting exercise to go through, as it forces you to look at the desired vertical shapes — the "surface" of the composition.

Like photographers and artists, designers have an eye for composition. If you analyze a composition — the way elements are arranged and framed — you'll find those concepts of balance, harmony, and repetition play a part in how the elements work together. Designers see lines and shapes, again looking for harmony, repetition, symmetry. They start with a concept, a framework, to which they then add details such as paths, flowerbeds, fences, and all the other specifics the client has requested.

When designers come to the point of adding plants to the basic framework, they will take into account the conditions of the yard: the type of soil, the amount of sun and wind, the zone, the purpose of the planting, the mature height and spread of the plant (something that's easy to forget!).

Drawing Up the Plan

You've now amassed quite a lot of information about your garden site and conditions and made some decisions about likes and dislikes. You understand some basic principles of design. Ideas are floating around in your head. Take advantage of that energy! Although they'll be pretty general at this stage, start sketching some of these ideas now. The details — especially the fun of choosing the particular plants — can come later. As your ideas gel, your plans will become more specific. But just before you put pencil to paper, you may be wondering whether you should use a computer or stick to good old paper. If you're not comfortable with a computer, I wouldn't recommend

If you find it hard to imagine what a mature planting will look like, study photographs in books and magazines. Better yet, take garden tours, with camera in hand. Reviewing scenes such as this will remind you of successful mature plantings and pleasing combinations of colour, form, and height.

rushing out to buy a landscape-design package. You won't use the package with the same frequency as a word-processing package, for instance, and may feel you never get your money's worth from it. In addition, you may not be pleased with the results, as the programs are not as flexible as pencil and paper and usually don't produce very realistic-looking results. However, if you're a gardener who also loves computers, don't let me put you off! You'll probably enjoy the challenge of learning the program, moving plants around, changing the view, and so forth.

So let's assume you're not going to use a computer. The basic supplies you'll need are paper, preferably grid paper, tracing paper or onionskin, pencils, and an eraser. You'll

notice I haven't mentioned a ruler. You'll need one to draw the boundaries of your site, or the portion of your yard you're designing. Once you've done that, put the ruler away. Unless you're attempting a formal garden, it's better to start out freehand, thinking about and drawing ovals and circles. Planning a garden by drawing squares and rectangles can result in a lifeless garden, so relax your drawing arm and start practising some loops! Other tools that are nice to have are coloured pencils, templates for drawing circles and ovals, and masking tape to attach tracing paper to master sheet.

Graph paper has the advantage of making measuring easier. Each square can equal a square foot or whatever scale that's easy to deal with. Make a master sheet by drawing in the outline of your plot and the main buildings and other permanent features — you can use the ruler to do this. Make the lines fairly dark, as this is a master you can use in a variety of ways. Add axis lines that mark the view from important windows and parts of the garden. Photocopy the master several times so you can try out several different designs before settling on the final arrangement.

Using the sight or axis lines from the house and outdoor seating areas, divide the space by sketching circles or ovals (if the garden is to be formal, you'll sketch squares and rectangles) to represent the main parts of the garden — play area, planting area, lawn, utility area, and so forth. Gradually add the details — patio, deck, paths, borders, fences. You're likely to want to wander to a window to remind yourself of what things look like or go outside to pace off and perhaps even mark some distances and shapes.

The greater the viewing distance, the greater the mass required to make an impact. Cluster like plants together according to the "visual size" you need to make the mass really effective.

At this point, you might want to put the plan away for a while and explore the ideas of colour, texture, and shape that I discuss in the next chapters. Once you've worked out the bones of a landscape design that satisfies your requirements — and carries out your dream — start having fun with colour. You won't be able to match the amazing variety Mother Nature provides, but at this stage you're interested in general colour schemes anyway. When you've finished the first part of this book, you have all the information to finish your landscape plans. Just as you sketched circles and ovals to start the bare bones of your design, grab your coloured pencils — or watercolours — and start colouring in swathes.

You've been working from a bird's-eye perspective up to now. If you're someone who has trouble visualizing from this view to a ground-level view, you may want to do more drawings, this time from a straight-on view. An advantage of this exercise is that you can sketch in the heights of plants to see how they blend in with the other elements and if they provide a feeling of equilibrium (remember the idea of being inside the Styrofoam block?). Another option is to take photographs of the garden and enlarge them on a photocopy machine. You can then mark all over them, paste on pictures of plants, furniture, statuary and other features to help in visualizing how it will all work.

I divide the process at this stage into what I call formal and informal. The formal part is creating the broad and sweeping lines and colours on paper or computer screen. Do not attempt to draw in annual flowers or perennial border plants at this stage. I always leave these until I am actually selecting plants at the garden centre. Your plan will include trees, shrubs, evergreens and significant structures such as gazebos, stairs, and decks. Colour should be indicated in blocks and clusters of shrubs, evergreens, or roses.

The day you select your plants will be very informal. At this time, I listen to my heart. I buy what I think will look good in my garden, using the plan as my guide. As a rule of thumb, choose several of one plant for an area unless the planting bed is very small or near a door, deck, or other closely viewed place. The point is that one plant, however colourful or attractive, will be lost when viewed from a distance greater than 3 m (10 feet).

As you can see, the exercise works from the very general — the macro view— to the micro — the plants. The plants will carry out your colour scheme, provide texture, and offer interesting shapes, all of which are dealt with in the next chapters.

The dappled light of a shady garden plays on the grass and provides ideal conditions for rhododendrons.

As you ponder being your own landscaper, you can see that you'll be changing hats frequently. Sometimes you're the horticulturist, sometimes the parent or pet owner, sometimes the artist, but bringing all these aspects together is challenging and fun. I started this book talking about planning and suggesting that planning a garden could be compared to planning a holiday. One of my favourite garden writers, Henry Mitchell, once wrote that gardening is a sort of travelling, "a kind of pilgrimage, you might say, often a bit grubby and sweaty though true pilgrims do not mind that." I also think that "true pilgrims" enjoy the travel as much as the arriving — in gardening terms, the planning and doing is often as rewarding as fulfilling the dream.

Change is one of the great benefits of gardening. Your final design will no sooner be "implemented" — installed and planted — than it begins to change. Colours, shapes, sizes, textures — all these elements of the garden are in a state of flux throughout each season and from year to year. It is this bonus — change — that draws ordinary people into the yard and, over time, changes them into gardeners, sometimes without them even knowing it.

3

Design Elements

It's important to understand some of the principles of colour, shape, and texture so you'll feel confident when you start to choose plants and furniture for your garden.

In Chapters 1 and 2, I discussed what could be called the macro aspect of garden design. It's the grand view, the overall, long-range plan implemented with plants, furniture, path surfaces, fencing materials. Now it's time to talk about the micro aspect — the details that will help convey the tone and feeling you want. In this chapter, I'm going to talk about the importance of colour, shape, and texture as you start to think of the details in your garden. These topics will recur later when I describe how to use hard and soft furnishings in your garden. But first it's important to understand some of the principles of colour, shape, and texture so you'll feel confident when you start to choose plants and furniture for your garden.

Look for colour, shape, and texture in the details, as well as in the large elements.

Principles of Colour

Some people just naturally seem to know what colours look good together and when to add a zinger, such as acid yellow or a difficult orange, to bring an arrangement to life. Others may feel they just can't get it right and don't know why. No matter which group you belong to, it's useful to understand something about basic principles of colour theory.

Often we take colour for granted. But there's that moment when you pause to appreciate a rose or a delphinium, and you're overwhelmed by the complexity of colours involved in making up what at first seemed a simple red or blue.

I like to think of plants as the paints we use to fill in the canvas that Mother Nature has provided us. Her canvas isn't static, either. It changes

day to day, season to season. Against that backdrop of greens and blues and blacks and browns, we set out our own palette. You'll probably find that you gravitate towards your favourite colours as you begin to leaf through gardening catalogues and books, and that's a good way to start. The process of choosing colours for your garden is similar to choosing colours for your walls, floors, and upholstery in your house or selecting the colours for your wardrobe. You start with colours you like, and whether you're aware of it or not, it's probably because those colours evoke an emotional response in you. There's a whole psychology of colour — painting offices certain colours, for example, can affect the productivity of the workers — but colour choice is highly individual, and the important thing for you as a gardener is to know which colours make you feel comfortable.

We sometimes feel uncertain about what goes together and what clashes. I sometimes advise people to plant containers with plants of varying single colours — an all-red one, all white, all yellow, and so on. Then observe how the colours look together. Move the containers around the garden to see what other combinations work. When you see which colours are compatible, you'll have the confidence to seek out and plant perennials and flowering shrubs with similar colours to your test plants'. It's a lot easier than digging plants up because you've made a mistake. In addition, by informing yourself about the principles of colour, you can confidently add colour accents to enhance the basic colour scheme you've chosen.

> When planning your colour combinations, don't forget to check the various blooming periods. If you want lovely deep wine tulips to bloom at the same time as the sunny yellow ones, make sure one type isn't an early bloomer and the other a late bloomer.

The Colour Wheel

The importance of the colour wheel, a handy way of classifying colours, for the gardener is not so much in helping you choose colours, but in understanding why some particular combination doesn't work. If you have a bland or jarring group of plants, sorting the colours out on the colour wheel can quickly tell you what's at the heart of the problem. Let's look at the colour wheel as a first step to understanding why some colour combinations don't work and why some surprising combinations do work.

The colour wheel is made up of twelve colours: three primary colours, three secondary colours, and six intermediate colours.

- Primary colours: Red, yellow, and blue, the primary colours, are the basis for all other colours. They are pure, lively, primitive, and demanding.

- Secondary colours: Orange, green, and violet, the secondary colours, are half-and-half mixes of two primary colours. Green is made of equal portions of yellow and blue; violet, equal portions of red and blue; orange, equal portions of red and yellow. They are fresh, exuberant colours.

These primary and secondary colours are arranged in a circle in the following order: yellow, orange, red, violet, blue, and green.

- Intermediate colours: These are obtained by mixing adjacent primary and secondary colours equally. Thus, yellow and orange give yellow-orange; orange and red give red-orange; the other intermediate colours are red-violet, blue-violet, blue-green, and yellow-green.

But what about the other colours — black and white and grey and all those other delicious colours that don't appear on the colour wheel? The colour of something depends on the percentage of primary colours and black and white that have gone into its makeup. You can see that white and black have an important role to play.

🍃 White mixed with any colour gives a pastel version of that colour, called a *tint*.

Colour can create a peaceful feeling: green is very calming; white provides a dash of purity; and violet is a colour that enlivens without overpowering.

🍃 Black mixed in gives a darker colour and is called a *shade*.

🍃 Black and white mixed together result in grey, and when grey is added to a colour, the colour is a *tone*.

These tints, shades, and tones are the colours that are of most interest to gardeners, for few colours in nature are primary. Especially important in the garden is the colour grey, or silver. I'll talk more about its use later in this chapter.

The colour wheel is frequently split into two general groups: hot and cool. The hot colours in the wheel are based on red and orange; the cool colours are those based on blue. The intermediate colours — those mixes of adjacent and primary colours — are linking colours and can be hot or cool, depending on how much red or blue is in the colour.

Plant annuals in containers — and move those containers around the garden — to change the effects you can get from your colour scheme.

If you put together a flowerbed or a hanging basket with plants that represented all the colours in the colour wheel, you'd have a real knockout! But would it be pleasing? No, it would be too much of a jumble. Pleasing colour arrangements are achieved by combining either harmonious colours or contrasting colours.

Contrasting and Harmonious Colours

Contrasting colours, sometimes called complementary colours, are any two colours opposite each other on the colour wheel. For example, yellow and violet are complementary colours, as are blue and orange and blue-violet and yellow-orange. These combinations are classic, vibrant, and pleasing. If the pure colours seem too strong, use them sparingly or use tints or tones — peach, rather than orange, with blue; lavender with pale yellow. Plants in a contrasting colour make wonderful accents and can have great value in the garden as a single specimen that sparks an otherwise lacklustre combination. But don't overdo it — just because one is good doesn't mean that several plants in one of these contrasting colours will be even better.

Harmonious colours are those that merge into each other in the colour wheel. Yellow, yellow-green, and green, therefore, are harmonious and can be used to give an effect that's soothing and sophisticated.

Using Colour for Effect

The choice of colours you use in your garden, whether for plants, fences, paths, or exterior walls, will have a profound effect on the feeling or mood of the garden. As I said earlier, you're likely to choose your favourite colours, the ones you're comfortable with, the ones that have an emotional resonance for you. But by using what you've learned about the colour wheel, you can confidently tone down a chaotic colour scheme or jazz up a dull one. Other factors affect how colour is perceived, as well. Here are some tips that are just a small sample of the magic that can be achieved by cleverly using colour.

- Blues, lavenders, and greys give a cool misty feeling.

- Cool colours such as green, blue-green, blue, blue-violet and violet make things appear farther away than they really are. A cool colour planted far from the house or sitting area will make the garden seem larger. Too far away, though, it can seem weak and hard to see.

- Hot colours — red, red-orange, orange, yellow-orange, yellow, and yellow-green — make things appear closer than they really are and are easy to see from a distance.

- Bright yellows and oranges can be difficult to incorporate with other colours, but some lovely effects are achieved by mixing in some white and purple.

- Bright colours planted just outside a window can make the room feel larger.

- Plants with variegated leaves of white or silver go well with a cool colour scheme. Plants with variegated leaves of yellow or gold are best in warm colour schemes.

- Brighten up a dull corner with a potted white begonia or impatiens.

- To tone down a strong colour, instead of using a neutral colour (cream, beige, tan, brown, silver, or grey), use a softer tint of the same colour. For example, the soft yellow of 'Moonbeam' coreopsis can tone down the clear primary yellow of sundrops.

John Weall, the founder of our family gardening business, used to say that a pansy always knew an attractive colour combination naturally.

Bright sun can wash out pale colours, and overcast skies can brighten them, intensifying pastels and light colours. With this in mind, you may want to put plants with pale blooms where they will be shaded from the bright noontime sun, which will severely wash them out. Let them catch the morning and late-afternoon sun to be seen to best advantage. I love the look of the new hostas that are in the gold range, especially one called 'Moonstruck'.

Bright sun can intensify bright colours and make them richer. Use this information when thinking about the garden in the spring and fall. Remember the shine of golden daffodils in the bright spring sun and how the deep jewel colours of tulips glow. Imagine the low autumn sun behind a rich red Japanese maple.

In shaded areas, pastel pinks, lavenders, and yellows glow, but burgundy, purple, and other dark shades fade into the gloom.

Fall is the time for strong and glowing colours. Take the strong blue-purple of ornamental cabbage and kale and mix them with variations on the theme — wine, burgundy, soft pink, and raspberry purple.

🍃 Sharp contrasts, whether of colour or texture, stop the eye as it travels along a bed; gentler contrasts keep the eye flowing.

🍃 About a third of the border or bed should be made up of greenery that mingles with the other colours. The green can come from the leaves of flowering plants or specimens used solely for their foliage.

🍃 You can achieve a feeling of full flowering with as few as 30 per cent of the flowers in a bed or border blooming at the same time if they are distributed throughout the bed in drifts rather than in one single clump. This is an important concept if you're attempting to achieve colour continuously from spring to fall.

Choosing a Colour Scheme

To me, one of the most natural and comforting colour combinations is blue and green. These colours reflect the very essence of the outdoors — sky, water, grass, and trees. But many gardeners are looking for variety, especially if you're someone who loves collecting plants, and who can always find another corner where one more specimen can be squeezed in. As you begin to sort out the micro details of your garden plan, you're getting a feeling for what you want your garden to convey. An effective colour scheme will help you achieve that goal.

Colour schemes can be broken down into four types:

🍃 monochromatic, which uses a single colour as the foundation for all plantings;

- cameo, which uses different tones of one colour and the colours closely allied to it;

- harmonizing, which uses simple colour combinations such as blue and white;

- contrasting, which uses complementary colours.

Monochromatic: Colour in flowers is quite complex — think of how many different kinds of green there are. In one plant, you will often find several shades of the main colour, even in white flowers. You can find everything from pure white, pinkish white, bluish white, silvery white, and cream. A monochromatic garden is not easy to carry off successfully, but it is stunning when done well. For the best effect, rely on textures and shapes to provide contrast and variety.

The most famous monochromatic garden is the white garden created by Vita Sackville-West at Sissinghurst Castle, in Kent, England. It could be fun to try your own mini version of Sissinghurst — but don't confine yourself to white. Make a green bed, or a violet bed, as an experiment. Practise with annuals if you don't want to go to the expense of perennials. Small gardens, in particular, can benefit from the monochromatic colour scheme; it helps you resist the urge to cram too many colours into too small a space.

Cameo: This is a fairly easy colour scheme to put together. Choose a "foundation" colour — a bluish pink, for example — then, using the colour wheel, select colours the foundation colour is related to. Bluish pink is an extremely accommodating colour, and most other pinks and blues will co-ordinate with

it attractively, as well as mauves and violets. A salmon pink, on the other hand, would need pinks in the orange-pink range.

Harmonizing: This is the easiest and most personal of all colour schemes to work out. Simply choose a colour combination, such as pink and white, or yellow, white, and burgundy. Use one of the colours — here's where white or grey prove their value — to separate the different shades, tints, and tones in the planting. If you have trouble deciding which colours to choose for this type of colour scheme, take a look at a favourite flower. For example, look at a pansy. There are usually two, sometimes three, colours on its flower, a ready-made colour scheme. Harmonizing also allows you to use many colours in the garden because you can progress from cool creams to brighter yellows, on to warm reds, oranges, purples, and blues.

Contrasting: The challenge in using contrasting colours is that they tend to produce bold combinations — remember that the contrasting pairs are red and green, blue and orange, and yellow and purple (or violet). The effect can be lost in an overload of colour. But it is possible to come up with some breathtaking combinations — just use them with care. Blue and orange, for example, are contrasting colours that can make a lovely combination. Try blue delphinium with orange calendula or blue flax next to an orange-bronze marigold. Another way of making contrasting colours work is to use a paler tint of one of the colours. Contrast can also be used in a larger way: use hot strong colours in one part of the garden in contrast to pale cooler areas.

The Colours

Let's get into a bit more detail about specific colours and their usefulness in the garden. The following sections discuss the different colours, with suggestions for plants to use in that colour range. If you're buying a plant that hasn't flowered yet — and this is frequently the case — you have to rely on the description tag or a picture. Even so, some experienced gardeners have been unpleasantly surprised when a plant turns out to be a completely different colour than expected.

As you plan your garden, think of yourself as a painter — with one difference. Instead of squeezing your colours out of a tube onto a palette, you'll be "painting"

Pink runs the gamut from pale to deep colour, where it begins to edge into wine. Yellow adds vibrancy. Note how the paler pink is shown off against a green background and the brighter colours are backed by white.

your garden with plants and their infinitive array of colour!

White

White in a garden gives the impression of space, as well as coolness, light, and tranquillity. As you study white plants, a new world opens up — white isn't just white any more. It's white with a rose flush, or tracings of green, mauve, or yellow.

Use white plants to make a transition between colours that might otherwise clash. White is a successful buffer between hot colours, such as yellow, and cool colours, such as pink.

To show off white flowering plants, set them against a background of dark evergreens. A garden with a lot of white is a wonderful nighttime garden. Annuals such as geraniums, pansies, and impatiens are easily obtained in white; planted in pots, they can be moved about when you want a hit of white in a particular spot. For spring, snowdrops will give an early white, and white varieties of crocus, hyacinth, and allium will continue it.

Pick up from your white plants colour echoes — that is, look at the details of the flower for veinings, blotchings, and spots that carry other colours. Use these hints of colour to choose colour companions. A daisy may be considered a white flower, but it has a yellow centre. That yellow can be echoed in other plantings such as yellow daylilies or poppies.

In a monochromatic white garden, silver foliage can set off white beautifully. The furnishings and decorations in an all-white garden should maintain the sense of serenity that white imparts, so choose dark greens and blues for paints and fabrics. Avoid too much white on tables, benches, and chairs, for it will detract from the plants.

Some of My Favourite White Plants
Perennials

🌺 Aster (*Aster ericoides*): flowers in summer and fall; blossoms are white to pale blue; full sun to partial shade in well-drained soil; 30 to 120 cm (12 to 48 inches). Zone 3.

🌺 Bellflower (*Campanula persicifolia* 'Alba'): flowers in spring and summer; blossoms are pure white and bell shaped; sun or partial shade in well-drained soil; 30 to 90 cm (1 to 3 feet). Zone 3.

🌺 Candytuft (*Iberis umbellata* 'Giant White Hyacinth'): flowers all summer to well into fall; delicate flower clusters are snowy white; full sun in average soil; 20 to 40 cm (8 to 16 inches). Zone 3.

🌺 Coral bells (*Heuchera brizoides* 'White Cloud'): flowers in spring and summer; hundreds of small white blossoms; moist well-drained soil in sun or partial shade; 45 to 90 cm (1 1/2 to 3 feet). Zone 3.

🌺 Delphinium (*Delphinium grandiflorum* 'Album' or 'Galahad'): flowers late spring and summer; white open blossoms; full sun for best results, rich, moist soil, dislikes acid soil; 1 to 2.5 m (3 to 8 feet). Zone 3.

🌺 Foamflower (*Tiarella cordifolia*): flowers in spring; blossoms are fuzzy white to pale pink spikes; partial to full shade in humus-rich slightly acidic moist soil; 15 to 25 cm (6 to 10 inches). Zone 3.

🌺 Goat's beard (*Aruncus dioicus*): flowers in late spring and early summer; blossoms are white fuzzy plumes; moist soil in partial shade; 90 to 180 cm (3 to 6 feet). Zone 3.

🌺 Lily of the valley (*Convallaria majalis*): flowers in early spring; blossoms are

---

You'll note that I haven't given zones for the annuals. Because they complete their life span in the growing season and die in the fall, you don't have to worry about their ability to withstand harsh winters.

white and fragrant bells; an underrated ground cover, insect and disease free, drought tolerant, and is competitive with tree roots; can become invasive; sun or shade, in many types of soil; 20 cm (8 inches). Zone 3.

🌼 Peony (*Paeonia lactiflora*): flowers spring to early summer; full, many-petalled blossoms are white and some are white flecked with red, depending on variety; full sun or light shade, in moist rich soil; 45 to 90 cm (1 1/2 to 3 feet). Zone 2.

🌼 Thrift (*Armeria maritima* 'Alba'): flowers from early to mid-summer; blossoms of this variety are white (other thrift varieties have vibrant pink, deep pink, or rosy-red flowers); full sun in average, well-drained soil; 25 to 35 cm (10 to 14 inches). Zone 3.

Try out a monochromatic garden on a small scale. To keep it interesting, look for contrasting textures and shapes, well illustrated here in the feathery shining astilbe and the rounded compact hydrangea.

Annuals

🌼 Nicotiana (*Nicotiana sylvestris*): flowers from early summer to fall; star-shaped trumpet flowers are white; partial shade, moist well-drained soil; 90 to 120 cm (3 to 4 feet).

🌼 Petunia (*Petunia*): flowers all summer, but keep out of wind if possible; wonderful in containers; a great range of whites and creams; the multifloras have smooth-edged flowers with a compact growth; full sun in well-drained soil. 20 cm (8 inches).

- Sweet peas (*Lathyrus*): flowers all summer, especially heat-resistant varieties; blossoms are creamy white ('Cream Southbourne'), deep cream ('Lilly Langtry'), snow white ('Royal Wedding'), swan's down white ('White Supreme'); sun but some protection from midday sun is advisable, well-drained soil; 1.5 to 4 m (5 to 6 feet).

Roses

- 'Blanc Double de coubert': vigorous shrub rose that makes a good hedge; blossoms pure white; deep green foliage; very fragrant; repeat flowering. Zones 2–3.

- 'French Lace': clusters of lightly fragrant creamy white blossoms; free-flowering ever-bloomer — one of my favourites! Zone 5.

- 'Mme Plantier': blossoms pure white; greyish green foliage; very fragrant; vigorous. Zones 3–4.

- 'Swan Lake': ever-blooming climber with medium fragrance; pure white clusters of flowers. Zone 5.

Shrubs and Small Trees

- Bridal wreath (*Spiraea*): flowers in late spring to early summer; blossoms can range from white to pink, so choose carefully; full sun in acid soil; to 2.5 m (8 feet). Zone 3.

Ornamental grass does triple duty. Its subtle blue-green is a great complement to other greens; it acts as a transition between low groundcovers and taller background plants; and its texture contrasts with flowing shapes of groundcovers.

The colour of this grass, miscanthus, looks good with blues, whites, and pinks.

Mock orange (*Philadelphus coronarius*): flowers in spring; blossoms are creamy white and very fragrant; full sun or light shade in well-drained soil; 3 to 3.5 m (10 to 12 feet). Zone 3.

Serviceberry (*Amelanchier canadensis*): flowers in very early spring (it's a wonderful harbinger of spring, but give it space!); blossoms are white and fragrant; tolerant of many soils; 2 to 6 m (6 to 20 feet). Zone 4.

Vines

Climbing hydrangea (*Hydrangea petiolaris*): perennial; flowers in early summer; blossoms are white, lacy, and scented; sun or shade in rich well-drained soil; 18 to 24 m (60 to 80 feet). Zone 5.

Moonflower (*Ipomoea alba*): annual twining climber; flowers all summer at night; blossoms large, white, and fragrant; full sun, rich porous soil; 2.5 to 3 m (8 to 10 feet).

Silver lace vine (*Polygonum aubertii*): extremely vigorous and fast grower — it is excellent at covering a pergola quickly; masses of small creamy white flowers from mid-summer until fall; tolerant of drought and poor soils, plant in full sun to partial shade; 7.5 to 10.5 m (25 to 35 feet).

Yellow

I think there's a reason daffodils are yellow — our eyes are aching for a bright splash of colour in spring, and yellow fills the bill. At any other season, this colour can appear a bit brassy, but in the spring it draws our attention away from the brown bare earth and a lawn recovering from winter, too. Both spring and autumn are seasons when yellow comes into its own, for those are the times of year when the sun is lowest in the sky and softens bright yellows.

Cheerful yellow looks best in a sunny spot, as it tends to lose its brightness in the shade. Too much yellow can be overwhelming to more subtle colours, but by choosing yellows ranging from cream all the way through to orange, you can give your garden a feeling of life and joy. It's a good accent, rather than the basis for a monochromatic garden, for which it could be too jarring.

Yellow flowers show off well against an evergreen hedge or a white fence or wall. Furnishings situated near yellow plants look best in pure white, light or dark green, or grey-blue. Accent flowers in that same range — white, sky blue, or deep purple — will complement the yellow flowers.

In addition to the ones listed below, other plants in the yellow-orange range include

primroses, wallflowers, poppies, and petunias. And don't forget foliage plants with yellow accents, such as many of the evergreens, hostas, and euonymus.

Some of My Favourite Yellow Plants
Perennials

🌼 Basket of Gold (*Aurinia*): flowers in spring; bright yellow small four-petalled blooms; looks great tumbling over a wall or in a rock garden; sun or light shade in fairly dry sandy soil; 22 to 30 cm (9 to 12 inches). Zone 3.

🌼 Butterfly weed (*Asclepias tuberosa*): flowers in summer; batches of small starry blossoms are fiery orange, yellow, or red; full sun in average soil; 30 to 90 cm (1 to 3 feet). Zone 3.

🌼 Daffodil (*Narcissus*): bulb; flowers in spring; trumpet blossoms are every colour of yellow from the palest cream

Don't hold back with strong colours such as yellow. Plant in masses for maximum effect rather than dotting plants here and there — they have more impact when grouped together.

to the deepest gold; 10 to 45 cm (4 to 18 inches). Zone 4.

🌼 Daylily (*Hemerocallis*): open-faced, wide-petaled flowers bloom from mid- to late summer; blossoms include colours such as glowing apricot ('Apricot Surprise'), red and yellow ('Fire Storm'), daffodil yellow ('King Alfred'), creamy yellow ('Going Places'); sun to part shade, well-drained soil; to 70 cm (28 inches). Zone 4.

🌼 Geum (*Geum*): flowers in spring and early summer; blossoms, flared or flounced, are yellow-orange (*G. coccineum* 'Georgenberg'), bright yellow (*G. quellyon* 'Lady Stratheden'); full sun to light shade in well-drained but moist rich soil; 30 to 60 cm (1 to 2 feet). Zone 4.

- Goldenrod (*Solidago canadensis*): flowers in summer and fall; blossoms are plumelike and bright yellow; full sun in average, well-drained soil, though will grow in a wide range of soils; drought tolerant; 60 to 150 cm (2 to 5 feet). Zone 3.

- Yarrow (*Achillea*): flowers in late spring through summer; tightly packed flat heads of tiny flowers are sulphur yellow ('Moonshine'), mustard yellow ('Cloth of Gold'), deep yellow ('Gold Plate'); full sun in average to poor well-drained soil; drought tolerant; 90 to 120 cm (3 to 4 feet). Zone 3.

Annuals

- Blanket flower (*Gaillardia*): flowers from spring to first frost; daisylike flowers with ragged edges are yellow to orange; full sun in well-drained soil, loves heat; 25 to 60 cm (10 inches to 2 feet).

- Marigold (*Calendula*): flowers all summer; neat rounded flowers from pale yellow to dark orange, depending on variety; sun; 30 to 60 cm (1 to 2 feet).

- Pansy (*Viola*): flowers from very early spring to summer; many colours, including some clear solid yellows and wonderful mixes all in the familiar appealing "faces"; full sun or shade in moist rich soil; 15 to 30 cm (6 to 12 inches).

- Snapdragon (*Antirrhinum*): flowers from early to late summer; many colours, including yellow and yellow mixes;

sunny location and will tolerate dry soil; to 45 cm (1 1/2 feet).

Roses

- 'Charles Austin': one of the outstanding members of the Austin roses from Britain; surprisingly hardy; apricot yellow with a heavy fragrance; grows to 1.5 m (5 feet). Zone 4.

- 'Double Delight': my all-time-favourite rose for cutting; hybrid tea with wonderful fragrance; creamy yellow blooms edged with red. Zone 5.

- 'Harison's Yellow': reputed to be the original "Yellow Rose of Texas"; blossoms gold yellow; mid-green foliage; scented; spring flowering shrub. Zone 3.

- 'Peace': one of the most popular roses; blossoms yellow edged with pink; green glossy foliage; slightly fragrant; blooms throughout summer; hybrid tea. Zone 5.

- 'Royal Gold': I have watched this climbing rose perform beautifully year after year; light fragrance, ever blooming. Zone 5.

- 'Sundowner': grandiflora with deep golden yellow and medium fragrance; leathery olive-green foliage; to 1.2 m (4 feet). Zone 5.

Shrubs and Small Trees

- Cinquefoil (*Potentilla fruticosa*): flowers throughout the growing season; blossoms bright yellow; full sun in well-drained soil; 30 to 120 cm (1 to 4 feet). Zone 2.

- Forsythia (*Forsythia* 'Ottawa'): flowers in early spring; blossoms are pale to bright yellow, depending on variety; full sun; 4 m (13 feet). Zone 5.

- Japanese kerria (*Kerria japonica*): flowers in early spring — great for cutting; blossoms are bright yellow; undemanding and tolerant of nearly any soil; full sun to partial shade; 1 to 2 m (3 to 6 feet). Zone 4.

- Laburnum (*Laburnum*): bears chains of yellow flowers in spring; light shade in moist well-drained soil; 3.5 to 9 m (12 to 30 feet). Zone 6.

Vines
- Black-eyed Susan vine (*Thunbergia alata*): annual; flowers all summer, with cream, orange, or yellow blossoms, with a purple throat; grows quickly and is a great addition to baskets and containers; full sun, average, well-drained soil; 2 to 3 m (6 to 10 feet).

- Clematis (*Clematis tangutica*): perennial; flowers summer to fall; blossoms are a rich buttercup that become silvery seed heads; doesn't need pruning; sun, rich, well-drained soil on the alkaline side; 3 to 4.5 m (10 to 15 feet). Zone 5.

- Honeysuckle (*Lonicera japonica* 'Aureo-reticulata'): perennial; flowers in spring; blossoms are white-yellow and fragrant; average garden soil in full sun or light shade; 9 m (30 feet). Zone 4.

Blue and Purple
There are definite purples and definite blues, but many blue flowers contain so much purple that I'm combining them under one heading. As well, because they make such pleasing combinations in the garden, it seems only natural to keep them together. In spite of that, some blues can fight with one another — pure blues, as seen in gentians, and purple-blues, as seen in many campanulas — and should be kept far apart. If you're detemined to have a wide variety of blues, put white and silver-grey plants between them to work as transitions. You can also mass some green-foliaged plants to separate warring blues. Good-looking accents are provided by yellow, orange, or scarlet flowers introduced here and there.

Furnishings and woodwork in colours of light green, white, or yellow look good with this colour theme.

Some of My Favourite Blue and Purple Plants
Perennials
- Balloon flower (*Platycodon grandiflorus*): flowers in summer; balloonlike buds open into star-shaped flowers that are bright blue, violet-blue, clear blue, or rich blue, depending on variety; also in white or pale pink; sunny position in light sandy soil; 45 cm (18 inches). Zone 3.

- Bearded iris (*Iris*): flowers spring and summer; blossoms are sky blue (crested iris), blue-grey (gladwin iris), deep blue to purple (reticulated iris), light violet (sweet iris); full sun to partial shade in well-drained soil; 15 to 90 cm (6 to 36 inches). Zone 3.

- Cranesbill (*Geranium*): flowers throughout summer, depending on variety; five-petalled blossoms are blue ('Johnson's

Creamy white and royal purple make a regal presentation in spring. On a practical note, plan for some fast-growing perennials to take over and hide the foliage as the bulbs finish blooming.

Blue'), as well as pink, white, or violet, depending on variety; sun to part shade, especially in afternoon; 30 to 45 cm (12 to 18 inches). Zone 4.

🌼 Delphinium (*Delphinium elatum*): my mother's favourite flower, it blooms in late spring and summer; blossoms dark blue ('Black Knight'), violet ('King Arthur'); full sun for best results, rich, moist soil, dislikes acid soil; 1 to 2.5 m (3 to 8 feet). Zone 3.

🌼 False blue indigo (*Baptisia australis*): flowers in spring; blossoms are blue with blue-green foliage; full sun to partial shade in average soil; 90 to 180 cm (3 to 6 feet). Zone 2.

🌼 Michaelmas daisy (*Aster novi-belgii*): lovely purple-blues for the fall garden; full sun in rich soil (lots of compost); 30 to 120 cm (12 to 48 inches). Zone 2.

🌼 Monkshood (*Aconitum napellus*): flowers late summer to fall; blossoms are blue, violet-blue, lilac, as well as white, yellow, or cream; partial shade in moisture-retentive soil; 60 to 180 cm (24 to 72 inches). Zone 2.

Annuals

🌼 Borage (*Borago officinalis*): flowers throughout the summer; blossoms are blue, purple, or white; average soil in full sun; 90 cm (3 feet).

🌼 Cornflower (*Centaurea*): flowers all summer; blossoms are lavender, deep blue, or bright blue, depending on variety, as well as white, pink, or red; sun, in poor to average soils; 30 to 70 cm (12 to 28 inches).

🌼 Forget-me-nots (*Myosotis*): self-seeding; flowers in spring; small delicate blossoms are bright blue or indigo blue, as well as white or pink; part shade in moist, well-drained soil; 17 to 30 cm (7 to 12 inches).

🌼 Heliotrope (*Heliotropum arborescens*): my very favourite for fragrance; purple-blue blooms; in full sun, rich moist soil; 45 to 120 cm (1 1/2 to 3 feet).

🌼 Larkspur (*Delphinium*): biennial; flowers all summer; blossoms are every shade of purple and blue, as well as some pinks and reds; porous well-drained soil and full sun; 30 to 120 cm (1 to 4 feet).

- Lobelia (*Lobelia erinus*): fabulous containers and hanging baskets; flowers most of the summer, though may need cutting back in mid-summer to encourage it to continue blooming; lovely delicate blue or purple flowers; can be used in partial shade; 20 cm (8 inches).

Roses

So far, no satisfactory blue roses have been created. The closest breeders have come is to a pink-lavender, bearing such names as 'Blue Moon' and 'Blue Jay'. I tried growing the latter around the time the Toronto Blue Jays won their second World Series — it was an utter disappointment.

Shrubs and Small Trees

- Butterfly bush (*Buddleia*): I call this shrub a butterfly magnet; flowers in late summer to late fall; blossoms are purple or blue, as well as burgundy, pink, or white; well-drained fertile soil in full sun to light shade; 1.2 to 4.5 m (4 to 15 feet). Zone 5.

- Rose of Sharon (*Hibiscus syriacus*): flowers mid to late summer; blossoms are in a range of colours, including purple and violet, but 'Oiseau Bleu' has blue flowers with a magenta throat; likes sun and well-drained soil; 2.5 to 3.5 m (8 to 12 feet). Zone 5.

Vines

- Clematis (*Clematis*): perennial climber; flowering times vary; blossoms are a mauve-white-pink mixture (*C. alpina* 'Willy', flowers in early summer), violet-blue (*C. integrifolia*, flowers in summer), indigo blue (*C. durandii*, flowers mid-summer to early fall); sun to partial shade in acid-free soil; 2.5 to 3 m (10 to 12 feet). Zone 2 for *C. alpina* 'Willy' and *C. integrifolia*, Zone 4 for *C. durandii*.

- Morning glory (*Ipomoea*): annual vine that flowers all summer; blossoms are blue-purple (*I. purpurea, I. tricolour*), rosy lavender (*I. tricolour* 'Wedding Bells'); average soil in full sun or light shade; 3 m (10 feet).

- Wisteria (*Wisteria floribunda*): perennial that makes a bold statement once it gets going — it needs strong support such as a pergola; the delicate-looking foliage and many clusters of violet-blue flowers are outstanding; full sun and well-drained soil; 9 m (30 feet). Zone 4.

Pink

As with all the other colours discussed in these pages, the single word pink cannot do justice to the many shades and permutations contained in this colour grouping. Pinks range from the palest blush to deep carmine. Even better, roses cover the spectrum, with delectable colours such as silvery pink, salmon pink, coral pink, clear pink, and pearly pink. Annuals such as geraniums also come in a wide range of pinks, among them orange-rose, salmon pink, coral pink, and blush pink.

You won't find pink on the colour wheel — it's made up of red diluted with white. Many pink blossoms blend naturally with plants bearing silver or grey foliage, but white, pale yellow, or lavender also make good companions. Pink looks great with stone, whether it's a wall, path, or boulder. Furnishings and garden accessories in silver-grey, pure white, or Prussian blue will complement rosy tones.

Colour and Texture

You can't really talk about colour and texture separately. The subtle gradations of green, for example, are often due to the different texture of a leaf's surface or a mass of ferny foliage.

Sun and shade play with green — and emphasize the texture of the fern's fronds.

Mother Nature provides the deep blue backdrop for the various purples of a columbine — in full flower and in bud.

This dahlia demonstrates the multitude of colours you can find in one bloom.

A classic colour combination — pink and silver. The round shape of the pink begonia flowers also contrasts with the more delicate silver dusty miller.

Even in decay, you can find beauty. The detail of the serrated edge, the mottled orange and black, won't be overlooked by the observant gardener.

Sometimes a visitor from the wild pops up in the flowerbed. Many insects are important pollinators; why not let them be?

Some of My Favourite Pink Plants
Perennials

- Anemone (*Anemone huphensis*): flowers in late summer to fall; blossoms clear pink with golden eye; sun to part shade in moist humus-rich soil; 50 cm (20 inches). Zone 5.

- Boltonia (*Boltonia asteroides* ' Pink Beauty'): flowers in late summer; blossoms pale pink; moist rich soil in full sun or light shade; 1.2 to 1.8 m (4 to 6 feet). Zone 3.

- Creeping phlox (*Phlox subulata*): flowers in spring; blossoms are various shades of pink (also in blue or white); average well-drained soil in full sun; 10 to 20 cm (4 to 8 inches). Zone 3.

- Hollyhock (*Alcea rosea*): biennial; flowers in summer; blossoms blush pink to carmine (also in yellow, white,

Worthy of an Old Master and perfect for the romantic garden. The transition from just-opened rose to fading bloom is captured here in one concise statement, as is the amazing variety of soft pinks.

deep red); full sun or partial shade in rich well-drained soil; 60 to 250 cm (2 to 8 feet). Zone 2.

- Meadowseet (*Filipendula palmata* 'Kahome'): flowers in summer; plumes of small blossoms bright pink on crimson stems; sun to partial shade in moist soil; 100 cm (3.5 feet); Zone 3.

- Poppy (*Papaver orientale* 'Carneum'): flowers in early summer; large cup-shaped blossoms are pink, salmon, flesh coloured; sunny well-drained spot; 60 to 90 cm (2 to 4 feet). Zone 2.

Annuals

🌸 Carnation (also called Pinks) (*Dianthus*): flowers from spring through the summer; grey-green foliage, mild clove scent, and array of various pink shades; plant in sun in well-drained soil; 15 to 30 cm (6 to 12 inches).

🌸 Cosmos (*Cosmos*): flowers summer to autumn; blossoms from pale pink to deepest pink (also in white, red, orange); average to poor soil in full sun; to 90 cm (36 inches).

🌸 Petunia (*Petunia*): flowers all summer, but keep out of wind if possible; wonderful in containers; rosy pink, salmon pink, cotton-candy pink — you can find a pink for any use; full sun in well-drained soil. 20 cm (8 inches).

Roses

🌸 'Tiffany': easy to grow; blossoms silvery-pink; olive-green foliage; fragrant; repeat flowering; hybrid tea. Zone 5.

🌸 'Camelot': good cutting rose; blossoms coral pink; glossy green foliage; spicy scent; repeat flowering; grandiflora. Zone 5.

🌸 'Pink Parfait': give afternoon shade to protect blossom colour; blossoms pink; medium green foliage; fruity scent; repeat flowering; grandiflora. Zone 5.

🌸 'Queen Elizabeth': said to be one of the world's most popular roses; vigorous grower, sometimes classified as a floribunda; blossoms clear pink; large dark-green foliage; faintly fragrant; repeat flowering; grandiflora. Zone 4.

🌸 'New Dawn': hardy climber; blossoms soft pink; dark green glossy foliage; scented; repeat flowering. Zone 5.

Shrubs and Small Trees

🌸 Azalea (*Rhododendron mucronulatum*): flowers in spring; blossoms are rosy purple; moist partially shaded spot in acid soil; 1.5 to 2.5 m (5 to 8 feet). Zone 5.

🌸 Dogwood (*Cornus florida* 'Apple Blossom'): flowers in spring; blossoms are light pink shading to white; full sun in neutral to acid soil; to 6 m (20 feet). Zone 5.

🌸 Flowering almond (*Prunus glandulosa*): flowers in spring; blossoms are pink or white; well-drained soil in full sun; 1.2 to 1.5 m (4 to 5 feet). Zone 4.

🌸 Rhododendron (*Rhododendron carolinianum*): flowers in spring; blossoms pink-rose to lavender; partial shade in acid soil; 90 to 180 cm (3 to 6 feet). Zone 5.

Vines

🌸 Clematis (*Clematis montana rubens*): perennial; flowers in early summer; blossoms are soft pink; sun to partial shade in acid-free soil; 2.5 to 3 m (10 to 12 feet). Zone 5.

🌸 Sweet pea (*Lathyrus*): annual; fragrant blossoms from spring to summer; pinks, as well as other jewel-like colours; plant in sun with support against a wall or fence or let scramble up a rustic obelisk; dwarf varieties to 37 cm (15 inches); tall to 1.8 (6 feet).

The red of Japanese quince can be hard to match with other reds. But underplant it with some late-flowering tulips in white and strong purple for a pretty picture.

Red

Red is a colour that can clash with itself, depending on whether it's a blue-red or an orange-red. And although pink is based in red, the two colours generally do not make good companions. Soften the effect of red with some white- and blue-grey-flowering plants and silver- and grey-leaved foliage plants. Dark red and maroon will tone down sharp scarlets.

Rather than trying to have a red garden from spring to fall (which can be quite tiring on the eyes and spirit!), concentrate on a red theme for the fall, when brilliant reds and yellows are naturally present in the landscape. The hot border created by an abundance of red will be quite striking as the sun lowers to an angle in the sky that strongly enhances the reds and yellows in the waning days of the gardening season.

A safe colour for furnishings and accessories in the red garden is white, but don't overlook dark green, red's contrasting colour, or a chocolaty brown.

In addition to the plants listed below, look to coleus for red foliage; gladiolus, begonia, dahlia, lily, zinnia, nasturtium, bearded iris, and chrysanthemum all have blossoms in many shades of red.

Some of My Favourite Red Plants
Perennials

- Astilbe (*Astilbe arendsii*): a long-lasting perennial; flowers in mid-summer; blossom plumes are dark crimson ('Fanal'), warm creamy coral ('Rheinland'); partial shade in moist soil; 45 to 120 cm (18 to 48 inches). Zone 4.

- Beebalm (*Monarda didyma*): blooms in summer; flowers are brilliant scarlet ('Cambridge Scarlet'), dark ruby red ('Mahogany'), red-violet ('Prairie Night'), reddish purple ('Violet Queen'); full sun to light shade, moist humus-rich soil; 60 to 120 cm (2 to 4 feet). Zone 4.

- Cardinal flower (*Lobelia cardinalis*): flowers summer and fall; blossoms are brilliant red; full sun to partial shade in constantly moist rich soil; 60 to 120 cm (2 to 4 feet). Zone 2.

- Maltese cross (*Lychnis*): flowers in mid-summer; blossoms are brilliant scarlet (*L. chalcedonica*), orange-red (*L.* x *arkwrightii*), or magenta (*L. coronaria*); full sun to light shade in average, moist well-drained soil; 60 to 90 cm (2 to 3 feet). Zone 4.

- Phlox (*Phlox paniculata* 'Starfire'): flowers in spring and summer; blossoms are a vibrant deep red, foliage is red tinged; full sun or light shade in average garden soil; 90 to 120 cm (3 to 4 feet). Zone 3.

- Poppy (*Papaver orientale* 'Beauty of Livermore'): flowers in early summer; large cup-shaped flowers are deep red; sunny well-drained spot; 60 to 90 cm (2 to 4 feet). Zone 2.

Annuals

- Celosia (*Celosia argentea plumosa*): flowers from mid-summer to frost; blossoms are bronzy red ('Apricot Brandy'), scarlet ('New Look'); full sun, rich well-drained soil; 25 to 60 cm (10 to 24 inches).

- Geranium (*Pelargonium*): flowers from spring to fall in scarlet to orange and every

Move colour around your garden when it's needed by planting up some containers. It's easy when you use lightweight materials such as this basket.

shade in between — look for names such as 'Scarlet Border' or 'Sensation Scarlet'; full sun and fast-draining soil; 25 to 30 cm (10 to 12 inches).

- Impatiens (*Impatiens*): flowers from spring to first frost; 'Bridal Passion' is a rich red — plant with a pure white for a true Canadian show; shade in rich soil; 15 to 25 cm (6 to 10 inches).

- Petunia (*Petunia*): flowers all summer, but keep out of wind if possible; wonderful in containers; not only can you get single-colour red petunias, but look for those that have white edges or creamy throats — use such combinations to pick up other accent colours; full sun in well-drained soil; 20 cm (8 inches).

Roses

- 'Blaze': popular climber; blossoms bright blood red; mid-green foliage; little scent; repeat flowering. Zone 4.

- 'Crimson Glory': protect from noonday sun; blossoms deep crimson; glossy green foliage; richly perfumed; repeat flowering; hybrid tea. Zone 5.

- 'Fashion': has a long blooming season; blossoms coral; olive green foliage; scented; repeat flowering; floribunda. Zone 5.

Containers

Use the colour of containers to help carry through a colour theme and enhance the beauty of the blooms and leaves. If the container is painted or decorated, echo the colours in the plants you choose.

Soft greys make many plant combinations look stunning, especially when one plant has blooms in a solid bright colour — think of masses of pale blue lobelia, some silvery helichrysum, and a clear red geranium.

- 'John Cabot': hardy climber that could also be grown as a shrub; blossoms deep red-pink; mid-green foliage; little fragrance; continuous flowering. Zone 3.

- 'William Baffin': hardy vigorous climber that makes a good hedge; blossoms medium red; mid-green foliage; little scent; continuous flowering. Zone 3.

Shrubs and Small Trees

- Japanese maple (*Acer plamatum*): foliage is wine-coloured in fall; slightly acid or neutral soil; filtered light preferred; 4.5 to 8 m (15 to 25 feet). Zone 5.

- Smoketree (*Cotinus coggygria* 'Royal Purple'): red "smoke" produced as flowers fade; purple leaves stay on through summer, becoming red in fall; tolerant of many soils but needs full sun; 2.5 m (8 feet). Zone 5.

- Sumac (*Rhus*): bright red foliage in the fall with orange-red fruits; light sandy loam in full sun; 3 to 6 m (10 to 20 feet). Zone 3.

Vines

- Morning glory (*Ipomoea*): annual vine that flowers all summer; 'Platycodon flowered Red' is a warm red, 'Relli-Valley' is a cherry red; average soil in full sun or light shade; 3 m (10 feet).

- Trumpet vine (*Campsis radicans*): perennial twining climber; flowers mid to late summer; blossoms are orange-red, attractive to hummingbirds; sunny spot, well-drained soil; 11 m (35 feet); Zone 4.

Green

The easiest monochromatic garden to put together is the green garden because there are so many beautiful foliage plants to choose from. Liven it up with plants with variegated leaves, and rely on texture and shape to provide the contrasts and interest. Try a green garden at the cottage — ferns and grasses will make a solid foundation on which to build. I believe that where a contrast of texture is desired, the most effective and varied family to choose from is ferns, especially in the shady garden. But the green garden can also be formal, with carefully clipped boxwood emphasizing a symmetrical layout. Yellow or blue flowers can complement the plantings if you feel the need for a break from green.

Garden furnishings should be white, deep brown, or deep green.

Some Selected Green Plants
Perennials

- Ferns: a large group, but valuable in any shady garden for the delicacy of their foliage, providing visual delights in both texture and shape; surprisingly, you can find a fern for just about any situation: male fern (*Dryopteris filix-mas*) will grow in many conditions, including dry shade; royal fern (*Osmunda regalis*) is also flexible in the conditions it requires, but in a bright damp area it will become very lush.

- Hostas (*Hosta*): another large group, hostas love shade but are not averse to sun, especially those with some green or yellow in their leaves; give them moist soil; hostas have a wide range of textures, too; *Hosta sieboldiana* has bluish green heart-shaped leaves, and some

cultivars have puckered leaves; the large leaves of *H. fortunei* are grey-green, but some varieties have leaves that are pale yellow with cream margins, green-edged gold, and dark green with a white border.

🌸 Lady's mantle (*Alchemilla mollis*): flowers in late spring; blossoms are acid green or chartreuse; foliage is downy and grey-green — it has the bonus of catching water droplets that look like small pieces of mercury nestled on its leaves; sun or shade, soil must be well-drained but moist; 30 cm (1 foot). Zone 3.

Sunlight can create entrancing effects — this astilbe glows against a dark background. It might be lit in this way for only twenty minutes a day — but what a twenty minutes!

🌸 Spurge (*Euphorbia griffithii*): flowers in summer; blossoms are orange-red; foliage is pale green; full sun to partial shade in well-drained, average to rich soil; 60 to 90 cm (2 to 3 feet). Zone 6.

Annuals

🌸 Bells of Ireland (*Moleculla laevis*): flowers all summer; blossoms are apple green, fading to a pale tan as they dry;

sun or partial shade in rich, moist soil; 60 to 90 cm (2 to 3 feet).

🌸 Coleus (*Coleus*): used mainly for its foliage of amazing greens — lime and chartreuse among others — as well as its deep and bright reds; shade to full sun, rich soil; 20 to 60 cm (8 to 24 inches).

Shrubs and Small Trees

🌸 Boxwood (*Buxus*): evergreen shrub; foliage is glossy green, responds well to clipping, and is slow growing; rich soil in sun or part shade; heights vary according to variety. Zone 4, depending on variety.

🌸 Hornbeam (*Carpinus*): small tree; foliage is ribbed and saw-toothed; slow grower, good in urban settings; sun or partial shade; can be used for hedging; 6 to 9 m (20 to 30 feet). Zone 4.

🌸 Yew (*Taxus cuspidata*): slow-growing evergreen with dark green needles; many uses — hedges, foundation planting, as a screen, on slopes; well-drained loamy soil in shade or sun; 3 to 12 m (10 to 40 feet). Zone 4.

Vines

🌸 English ivy (*Hedera helix*): evergreen perennial creeper/climber; lustrous dark green with white veins; rich moist and well-drained soil, full sun, where it will grow more profusely, to full shade; to 27 m (90 feet). Zone 4.

🌸 Euonymus (*Euonymus*): a large group of evergreen plants with shades from shiny dark green to light green, to variegated; leaves often change colour during the season; useful in many situations, prefers sun but will tolerate shade; responds to clipping; tolerates many soil types. Zone 3.

Silver and Grey

Silver and grey plants can be used to create a tranquil effect in the garden, but they're also invaluable as transitions and as calming foils for bright, hot colours. They tend to prefer sunny areas and many are drought tolerant.

Some of My Favourite Silver and Grey Plants

Perennials

🌸 Artemisia (*Artemisia*): long slender silver grey-white leaves; full sun, average well-drained soil; many varieties in sizes from 30 to 120 cm (1 to 4 feet). Zone 2, depending on variety.

🌸 Lamb's ears (*Stachys byzantina*): flowers in spring and summer; blossoms are small pinky grey; foliage is woolly and silver; average to rich moist well-drained soil in sun or partial shade; 15 to 35 cm (6 to 14 inches). Zone 4.

🌸 Pearly everlasting (*Anaphalis margaritacea*): flowers in late summer; blossoms are papery white with yellow centres; foliage is grey-green; semi-shade in any soil with good drainage; 30 to 90 cm (1 to 3 feet). Zone 3.

🌸 Russian sage (*Perovskia atriplicifolia*): flowers in summer; small blossoms are lavender; stems white, smoky grey pungent felty leaves; full sun in well-drained soil; 90 to 120 cm (3 to 4 feet). Zone 4.

🌸 Santolina (*Santolina chamaecyparissus*): flowers in summer; blossoms are small,

The contrast of textures and shapes — smooth, tall tulips with a low-growing ground cover — provides a harmonious combination.

deep yellow, button shaped; pale silver-grey foliage; average to poor soil in full sun; 30 to 60 cm (1 to 2 feet). Zone 5.

Annuals

- Dusty miller (*Senecio cineraria*): flowers in summer; blossoms are insignificant, yellow or cream coloured; foliage is felty grey; sun, well-drained soil; 60 cm (2 feet).

- Licorice plant (*Helichrysum petiolatum*): furry leaves, grey on one side, silvery on the other; good in sunny exposed conditions, by the sea, and in containers where the arching, sprawling stems will spill over the edge; 90 cm (3 feet).

Shrubs and Small Trees

- Arctic willow (*Salix lanata*): foliage is bright green to silver green; moist soil in full sun; 1.2 m (4 feet). Zone 1.

- Russian olive (*Elaeagnus angustifolia*): silver foliage; attractive shredding bark in winter; drought and wind resistant; full sun or light shade; 6 m (20 feet). Zone 2.

Texture and Shape

I first really became aware of the variety of leaf textures and shapes when I helped one of my kids with a school project — putting a piece of paper over a leaf and rubbing it with a crayon.

Texture and shape are important components in the garden. The terms texture and shape can apply to many things in the garden. Texture can refer to ground cover (grass or some other plant); the material of paths and decks; the background material (plants, walls, fences, and so on); the foliage and flowers of the plants. Shape can refer to the shape of a tree or plant or the shape of a leaf, flower, or paving stone. Using texture and shape with colour, we can create harmony by echoing colours and shapes, as well as introduce the valuable concept of tension by creating contrasts.

Texture

Let's look at texture first by examining a hosta. This one simple plant can provide a great range of textures and colours, depending on the varieties you plant — the foliage may be a puckered green-blue, a ribbed deep blue, a glossy shiny green with yellow margins, an ice blue and lance shaped, and then there are the many matte finishes we find on hostas. Such plants grab attention.

These bold plants can seem heavy and be overpowering if used too frequently, especially in small spaces, but they can make a great focal point and provide needed contrast.

Most plants fall between the two extremes of bold and fine textures. Finding the right balance is a challenge — too many varied textures and the effect is jumbled, busy, and jarring; too much sameness and the effect is boring and lifeless. Assess the plants you want to use together in a bed or setting. What is their overall shape? What are the shapes of the leaves? Is the foliage matte or shiny? Is the leaf one colour on top and another underneath? What is the mature height and spread expected to be? If your border is a perennial one, texture becomes an important consideration, for most perennials have a rather short flowering period, but their foliage will be on display for the whole season.

Using fine-textured plants such as maidenhair fern can take some skill and practice to present to their best advantage. They seem to recede from view; because they may look smaller than they really are, they can make a small area look bigger and more restful.

Using a variety of textures in the flowerbed will provide contrast, another important design concept. Observe plants closely, especially foliage plants, and think about the many ways these plants can be used in the garden to provide contrast. As you study shape and texture, you'll begin to see plants slightly differently — as a designer rather than a plants person.

Another aspect of texture is what's left when the plant's leaves fall or die in autumn. Although a plant's leaves may be fine textured and lacy, such as a cutleaf sumac's, the bare trunks and limbs may be thick, coarse, and rough. These are important features in the winter when the textures and skeleton shapes of plants are exposed.

Consider too the texture of your furnishings — the decks, paths, fences, containers, benches, tables. Wood can be painted to be shiny and smooth or left to weather naturally, with a soft matte texture. Stones have textured surfaces, but concrete pavers may be quite smooth. Pebbled paths have a different texture from mulched paths. There's texture in tabletops, umbrellas, and cushions, but try not to introduce too many highly textured objects or you'll end up with a busy and overwhelming feeling. If you've got one bold texture, choose materials and plants that will complement it rather than fight with it.

Shape

If you've already started on your design, sketching things out, scribbling ideas on the

---

Shape Tips

To show off the shapes of large trees and shrubs to best advantage, keep them uncluttered; don't plant something nearby that will interfere or compete.

Choose a tall plant as the focal point in a planting, and surround it with plants of lower growth habit and complementary shape. For example, rounded shrubs can be tucked under the arching branches of a vase-shaped tree. They will fill the spot without competing against the larger tree's shape or interfering with its growth.

An exuberant combination of annuals and perennials in a variety of forms gives an overall impression of roundness in the foreground, rising to more vertical shapes in the background.

backs of envelopes, you've already begun to consider the question of shapes — ovals, squares, circles, rectangles, triangles. Novices seem to feel happier grabbing a ruler and squaring everything off when they sit down to plan a garden. In some cases, this is the best way to start. To others, though, more relaxed curved shapes will suit the setting best. Look to your landscape and existing exterior architecture to guide you. In the first chapter I talked about echoing shapes, and if you're having trouble getting started, this can be a real inspiration. In an urban setting,

many of the existing shapes will be geometrical — straight lines, angles, circles. In a rural area, the existing shapes may be found in nature — rolling hills, flat prairies, sheer granite cliffs, the curves of sand dunes, or the zigzag of mountains on the horizon. Use these visual resources as you begin to sketch your garden plans.

Decide whether you want to echo existing shapes or begin a new theme. As just one example, paving stones come in a huge selection of shapes and textures, but once you begin to refine your plans and focus on the feeling you want to convey, you focus quickly on your favourites.

4

Garden Furnishings

Furnishing a garden with non-plant embellishments is no different from furnishing an apartment or house. Put your thumbprint on the garden with interesting additions that tell stories and at the same time serve a practical purpose.

"Furnishing" your garden — adding non-plant embellishments — is the perfect way to tell stories about you and your family. Consider all the wonderful items you see during your vacations, the many locally handcrafted items that are available. Around my yard you'll find a clay toad house from Cobourg, Ontario; a hand-knotted rope hammock from Truro, Nova Scotia; a 30 cm (12-inch) copper rabbit from a favourite garden centre in Minneapolis; a "re-tire" swing horse for the kids from Muskoka, Ontario.

If you take a walk with me through my garden, we'll need lots of time because I get so caught up as I relate stories about the people and places associated with my garden furnishings. In this chapter, I suggest you personalize your garden even further. Put your thumbprint on it by way of interesting additions that tell stories and at the same time serve a practical purpose.

Do you remember the first apartment you had? Or what you began to think about when you walked in the front door of your first new house? You can likely recall the feeling of ownership for your own space and how you wanted to put your stamp on it. You probably wanted to change things to reflect your personal style and tastes.

Furnishing a garden is no different from furnishing an apartment or house. I talked in Chapter 2 about the concept of rooms in the garden, and

An enticing view, framed by a sturdy and attractive fence. The statue rises from a sea of daylily blades — and we can't help wondering what's just around the corner.

Containers shouldn't overpower the plants growing in them, so soft subtle colours are best. If a container is truly stunning on its own, show it off as a focal point — don't overdo it by adding plantings that will compete with it.

that idea makes abundant sense when you start to think about the floors, walls, and roof of your garden rooms.

The roof can be open to the great blue sky, but a bit of shelter is nice — shelter in the form of a partially covered deck, a romantic gazebo or pergola, or the shade of an arching branch. The floor can be a combination of grass, paving stones, brick, with halls (in the garden we call them paths!) in a contrasting material. Consider the outdoor walls of your house and garage as "indoor" walls of the garden rooms, with other walls constructed of formal or informal hedges, trellises and vines, fences, or anything else that can be thought of as a wall.

Many of the larger items of "furnishing" — the paths, driveways, fences, and gates — should be high on your list of what to do first. These large jobs will cost more, cause

more disruption, and take longer if they are done after the sodding, the bed preparation, and the planting. If you're implementing your plan over several years, these basic and important items should be done in Year 1.

Once you have the bare walls and floor sketched out, it's time to start thinking about furniture — chairs and tables, for sure, but a garden offers many more opportunities for furnishings, such as gazing globes, birdbaths, sculpture, and more. There's lighting to consider, for decorative as well as security purposes, and how to arrange eating areas. As you refine your ideas and get down to the specifics, you'll be referring to your notes, drawings, and photographs as you select the accessories that carry out the theme you've chosen for your garden.

Decks and Patios

Decks and patios make good transitions from indoors to outdoors, a job performed in the past by porches at the front of the house and a stoop at the back. Today, decks can be rather grand affairs, combining planters, barbecue areas, sitting areas, even water gardens. It's easy to plan for storage areas to be incorporated when you draw up your plans. Keep the deck in proportion to the house and property so it doesn't overwhelm either, and carry through the style you've chosen or that reflects the architecture of your house. If you are adding a deck to an existing house, it's hard to avoid the impression that the deck has had a forced marriage with the house, but some fast-growing plantings will help to soften the newness.

Decks can solve house-garden access problems for properties that slope,

Paving Stones

A well-laid interlocking brick patio, walkway, or drive-way needs at least 15 cm (6 inches) of excavation and three layers of limestone screening; each layer must be tamped with a mechanical tamper. It's a job you're likely to leave to a professional — but if you do, you may find you get a great variation in quotes. The difference often has more to do with the preparation than anything else.

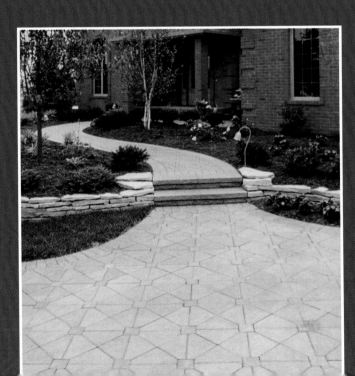

Combining various materials — wood, stones, bricks — for paths and patios can add interest in their contrasting textures, shapes, and colours.

providing an easy means to move from the house to the garden, as well as a spot from which to view the garden. A second-floor or roof deck, or one that will have stairs to a lower level, needs to meet requirements for loadbearing. To ensure stability, the deck will have to be supported by piers set in concrete footings. You may have to consult with a structural engineer or architect to be sure you will not be causing damage to the structure of your house.

Patios and decks can be constructed from traditional materials such as wood, stone, and brick, but new products are coming on the market all the time, so visit a building supply centre to see the latest products.

Wood: Wood is a natural for decking, and it's relatively easy for the handy homeowner to build a deck with wood. But review the conditions the deck will face. If it is in an unprotected area where it will stay damp for lengthy periods, the deck will need extra attention — frequent treatments with protective stains, for example. If children will be running on the deck, slivers can be a problem, so finishing the wood well and keeping it in good repair will be important.

The best woods for decks are the weather-resistant ones such as redwood, cypress, cedar, and pressure-treated woods, though care must be taken when working with the latter; this lumber is treated with a toxic material and you should take precautions when working with it, such as wearing a dust mask. These woods are more expensive than pine, spruce, hemlock, and Douglas fir, which also make good, serviceable decks. No matter which type of wood you choose, you can't get away from the fact that it

needs upkeep such as staining and waterproofing treatments over the years, but a deck that has received consistent care will give many years of use.

Wood has many advantages. It's relatively inexpensive, it lends itself to a great variety of designs, and it's light in weight compared with bricks and stones, so it's ideal for roof gardens. Not only can wood be painted

just about any colour you want, but it can be laid down to make attractive patterns.

Bricks: Constructing a brick patio is another easy job for the do-it-yourselfer, easier than building a deck, especially if no mortar is used. In the colder parts of Canada, where the frost penetrates the ground deeply in winter, a patio laid without mortar will bet-

This creative wall separates the garden into different rooms and gives privacy. The round openings serve a practical purpose too — they increase air movement but just as importantly, they offer an enticing hint of what lies beyond.

ter withstand the shifts and heaves caused by freezing and thawing. On the other hand, mortar can add to the appeal and attractiveness of the patio — it can complement the colour of the brick and will emphasize the pattern you've chosen for laying the bricks. (It also eliminates future weeding problems.) Purchase bricks specially made for patios and walkways, as they should not crack during the winter. Although regular bricks are quite attractive, especially if they are a bit aged, they will not last for more than a couple of years before starting to crumble as a result of the constant exposure to traffic and moisture.

New bricks can look at bit raw at first, before they've had a chance to weather and have their edges softened by creeping plants planted between them. Interlocking

The best paths are not laid out in straight lines. This weathered brick has a soft texture and is designed to be fairly unobtrusive. Note how nicely the colour of the path and the shrub work together.

bricks come in a wide range of shapes and colours, with some pleasing soft greys and buff colours that seem to look at home right away. Some manufacturers provide clear and detailed instructions on how to lay them.

Depending on the use of the patio, it will be important to have a smooth and even surface — there's nothing more irritating than a wobbly table that sends your lemonade sloshing!

Flagstone: Since it is a natural material, stone complements garden plantings, but it takes some skill and aesthetic sense to lay a satisfactory patio with stones. Generally they are irregular shapes, so it takes time to decide the best way to arrange them, but it can be time well spent.

Purchase locally quarried stone if possible — it will be cheaper than other stone and will look more at home with your plantings and soil.

Running bond pattern looks good with modern architecture.

Mortared herringbone has an old-fashioned country look.

Stones have an uneven surface and their thickness may vary, making it challenging to produce a smooth surface, so they're not always appropriate for a patio that will be used for an eating area, unless the furniture is placed on a smoother more stable surface. Mortaring the stones will stabilize them, but the surface may still be uneven.

Precast Cement Pavers: I've seen some clever cement paving stones that bear little resemblance to the more usual square pavers. They come in a range of colours and with various surface finishes — non-slip finishes are important in areas around swimming pools and spots that tend to stay damp for prolonged periods. Cement paving stones are easy to install, require little upkeep, and are relatively inexpensive. They're appropriate to use in barbecue and utility areas, but unless chosen with great care and kept to small sizes, they are not very attractive in a romantic or cottage garden. Cement pavers have clean lines and their shape can be used to great advantage in a modern setting, especially if they echo the lines and angles present in other constructions such as seating, raised flowerbeds, and streamlined architectural gates, fences, and trellises.

Paths and Walkways

Though primarily utilitarian, paths and walkways become important parts of the design, tempting the visitor farther into the garden, leading him or her into secret sections of the garden, guiding people away from less attractive parts of the property. The path directs your steps, controlling your movement through the garden. It should have a purpose, so plan its placement carefully and thoughtfully. A meandering path should meander for a purpose, to a bench or stand of shrubs or small trees, and not wind in an aimless way across an open lawn. Let it take your steps to a reward — a seat, a view, a hidden surprise.

There is more diversity in the materials that can be used for paths and walkways than for decks and patios. However, wood, brick, and stone can be used and the same concerns apply — stability, smoothness, use, and upkeep. If you're an active gardener, ferrying loads of compost back and forth in a wheelbarrow or regularly moving a lawnmower from one part of the property to another, the paths you use need to be firm and stable and for these situations, brick (and I include interlocking brick), cement pavers, or wood are often the best.

In a yard where most of the grass has been taken up to make room for flowerbeds and a patio or deck, some grass can be left to mark the paths. It will be cool and comfortable to walk on, but in a heavy-use area it will wear down quickly. It will need to be mowed occasionally and special attention may need to be paid to the edging between the path and the flowerbeds.

Other natural paving materials to consider include pea gravel, crushed rock or stone, flagstones, slate, and bark chips. In regions of cold snowy winters, materials such as pea gravel, crushed rock, and bark chips are not practical for walkways that need to be kept clear in the winter. As well, they can all prove difficult for walking on, and weeds will make an attempt to grow, sometimes with amazing success. But it's hard to imagine a woodland garden that doesn't have a bark-chip path, and some people love the satisfying and evocative crunchy sound of footsteps on pea gravel or crushed rock. Gardeners on the coast of British Columbia, including the coasts of Vancouver Island, can quite safely plan to use crushed rock or gravel and even tiles for their paths. Their infrequent snowfalls need not be a restriction when choosing paving materials.

Some other points to keep in mind when planning paths and walkways:

- Good drainage is vital, so the path should be a bit higher than surrounding beds and lawns so it will dry quickly after rain and not collect water.

- If children and elderly people will be using the path, build it of a smooth, non-slip material. The materials should be firmly set, with no gaps between sections. It would be advisable not to let plants creep into the walking area.

- Consider upkeep when planning the path. Stones or concrete pads set into grass will need special attention at mowing time to keep the grass growing at the edges well clipped.

- A formal garden usually has paths set out in a symmetrical fashion. Informal gardens use curving, free-flowing shapes for paths and borders. However, even a formal layout can be given an informal feeling by allowing plants to creep and spill into the path area.

- Generally, a path should be wide enough to accommodate two people walking side by side, at least 1 m (3 feet).

Fences, Walls, and Gates

Fences, walls, and gates — the equivalent to walls and doors in a house — keep people and animals out, and they give a sense of privacy and peace to a garden. They also provide yet another way to express your garden style, so you should keep this in mind when choosing the material for fences and walls. A rustic rail fence is appropriate in a cottage garden, and a wrought-iron fence looks better in a more formal garden. In addition, a fence or wall can have a purpose other than exclusion, of course. A waist-high fence or wall can separate two parts of the garden, provide a backdrop for a cherished plant or piece of furniture, break up a large open space, provide seating, surround a patio, or show off a favourite flowering vine.

The material that can be used for fences and walls is practically limitless: wood, wrought iron, cement breeze blocks, lattice of all types, bamboo screening, stone, brick, even plants, and within each of those categories, the designs and styles available are almost overwhelming.

Before planning or building a fence, check with your municipality about height restrictions. As well, there are sometimes specifications for the amount of airflow that passes between fences, so if you want to install a solid fence, be sure you're not breaking a bylaw. If you're sharing the cost of a fence with your neighbour (and therefore agree on the design, materials, and so forth), the fence can be built right on the

Flagstones are a natural choice for formal and informal paths.

property line; if you can't agree with your neighbour on the style and cost of the fence and want to go it alone, you can build it 2.5 cm (1 inch) inside your side of the property line. As you modify and clarify your landscaping plans, check these matters out — better to do it now than when you've got the fence partly constructed.

A good-neighbour wooden fence is the type with a base stringer running the length of the boundary and the planks are nailed to each side alternately, making a fence that has no right or wrong or good or bad side. However, if you end up on the "wrong" side of a new fence, use it to your advantage: grow vines over it, attach pots to it, cover sections in lattice, attach shelves to it.

A tall fence or wall around a small area can make the garden seem somewhat claustrophobic, but clever plantings will help to soften the impact of the boxed-in feeling. Some fences are meant to mark boundaries as well as carry through the theme of the

Soften the "stay-out" feel of a fence with a fast-growing vine. Privacy is maintained, boundaries are marked, but you share the beauty of the plant with your neighbours.

garden rather to than provide privacy. Picket fences and wrought iron fences are two examples of such fences.

In some situations, you may find you need to install chain-link fencing, just about the least attractive fencing around. However, it is cheap, easy to install, and relatively long lasting. Disguise it with climbing plants — if one of them is evergreen, so much the better, since unadorned chain link looks no more attractive in winter than in summer. You can also attach sheets of bamboo reeds to it. The bamboo will need to be replaced every few years, but it's inexpensive, attractive, easy to install, and gives an interesting texture.

Wooden fences can be designed to fit into nearly every garden style, from Japanese gardens to wildflower gardens to formal rose gardens. Treat wooden fences with a preservative (not creosote, which can damage plants) or paint them. In order to prevent rotting, the palings (planks) should not touch the ground. The tops of the palings can be finished with a decorative cut or left square or rounded.

Building supply centres carry ready-made fencing sold by the panel — a quick and easy way to install a fence. Lattice panels are an attractive way to hide an unsightly view and have many other advantages and uses: to provide privacy, allow air movement, act as a trellis, or finish off the gap between a deck and the ground.

Constructing a wall is a bigger job than installing a fence and usually makes a much more definite statement. If it is an extension of the house, it should be constructed of the same material as the house. Such walls often make little "suntraps" — places that warm up quickly in the spring and stay warm well into the fall, creating enticing corners for a little table and chair, a place to sit and relax. A pot of daffodils and crocuses in the spring or chrysanthemums in the fall adds to the ambience of a suntrap.

Walls can be constructed of stone, concrete or concrete block, brick, or railway ties. If you're using stone, a local one gives a more natural look as it will fit in with the soil and natural plantings in a more pleasing fashion. Limestone and sandstone are easy to handle. Concrete looks best when a specially formulated stuccolike surface is applied, though this may require some upkeep if you paint it. A brick wall, which can be expensive to have constructed and requires skill on the part of a do-it-yourselfer, does not make as strong a wall as stone or concrete. If you want a brick wall more than 90 to 120 cm (3 or 4 feet) tall, the inner core will have to be built with concrete and bricks used as a facing.

Human nature being what it is, once we get a wall built, we want to cover it up — it's like a blank canvas waiting for some paint. Good plant "paints" for blank walls include such climbers as bittersweet, clematis, climbing hydrangea, silver lace vine, wisteria, trumpet vine, Boston ivy, and English ivy. Not all these will cling to the wall but may need supports such as trellises or poles to twine themselves around.

Alternatively, a hedge or screen provides special benefits that a wall or fence can't match. Just as walls do, hedges enclose, protect, offer privacy, provide shelter, hide an unattractive view, define spaces, and so forth. They're also flexible. Left unpruned, they're free flowing and informal. Clipped closely, they're more formal, a perfect backdrop for showing off specimen plants, figurines or sculptures, or furniture. A hedge requires annual pruning but provides a cool addition to any yard.

The plants can be planted in a straight row, in a curve, or to go around corners. The hedge can be tall or short, it can have openings clipped into it, it can have a scalloped top, or it can be combined with walls, fences, and gates to fill in where a separation is desired. It's easier to plant a hedge on a hillside than it is to build a wall or fence. In a large garden, a hedged corridor can direct the eye to a piece of sculpture or specimen plant situated at its end. A hedge also makes the perfect enclosure for a "secret garden" —

a place not visible from any other part of the garden.

A gate can be set in a wall, a fence, or a hedge. The gate design should carry through the design of the feature it's attached to, even if it's constructed of different material. For example, in a country garden, a rustic wooden gate could be set into a stone wall. Wrought-iron gates are more formal and would look at home in a sharply trimmed hedge. Unless its purpose is to give total privacy and security, a gate that allows the passerby a glimpse into the garden provides a desirable sense of allure and mystery.

The gate's frame must be well constructed to allow it to close properly. Diagonal cross braces in a wooden gate will ensure that it will not sag and can be used as a design feature. Decorative hinges and other hardware add an individual touch to your gate. If you can't find what you want at the hardware store, seek out someone who works with wrought iron or other metal to produce what you want. You can also hire a carpenter to build you a gate that you have designed. Many skilled artisans will take on such commissions, and you'll have a one-of-a-kind addition to your garden. The gate should be well supported by its hinges and support posts, especially if there are children about — for them, there's nothing better than swinging on a gate!

Steps

Are you one of the lucky gardeners who has a sloping site or one that has different grades? You're lucky because not only do varying grades make a garden more interesting, but also you get the chance to install some steps and make them a feature.

- If you make them wide enough, you can set pots on the steps or use them as seats.

- Steps can be constructed of the same materials as patios and decks, which they should match.

- Shallow steps are inviting, lending themselves to a garden setting.

- Steps don't have to go straight — they can be staggered, irregular, or angled. They can also have a landing, where they turn.

- If the steps will be in everyday use throughout the year, drainage is important. Wooden steps with space between the boards will allow water to drain. The front edge of stone or cement steps should slope down slightly to let water run off; small gutters can be built in to direct the water to the edges, as well. Water should not collect on the tread where it could freeze or become slippery.

Arbours, Pergolas, and Gazebos

Building any of these structures in your garden is a bold undertaking, but careful planning, which is essential, will ensure it is a successful addition to your garden. Generally, a pergola or arbour will look as if it belongs if its introduction has solved a problem, such as how to separate garden rooms, rather than been added simply because you've always dreamed of having one.

An arbour is a covered place to sit in or pass through from one part of the yard to another. It may or may not have vines growing over it.

A pergola is an arbour used to support vines or shrubs growing over a trellis or latticework and creating a series of arches that cover a path.

A gazebo is a small building that usually contains comfortable furniture.

As you assess your garden and its potential for a pergola, arbour, or gazebo, take the following into account:

- Scale: The finished size must be in keeping with the size of the garden.

- Proportion: The design should be pleasing — the height must not be too high for the width and vice versa.

- Style: The design of the structure and the plantings that will adorn it must continue the theme of your garden— an ornate Victorian gazebo would look out of place surrounded by the minimalist plantings of a Japanese garden.

Take advantage of slopes — with a dramatic set of steps, for example. It's important that they offer good footing.

Garden Furnishings

These are the additions that make your garden different from everyone else's. You don't need a lot of them — in fact, too many will lessen the impact. Use them as focal points or pleasant surprises peeking out from shrubbery. Those made of material that withstands cold weather will gain extra prominence in the winter as snow catches in crevices and curves that are invisible in the summer.

Choose the furnishings for your garden that are appropriate to its style. The half whiskey barrel and simple birdhouse are at home in an informal setting. Ornate statuary and urns are more suitable for gardens with a formal air but each could be used as a focal point in any garden if other garden furnishings are kept to a minimum.

Generally, arbours have some kind of framework, often incorporating a trellis, with a roof of some sort. Even the smallest arbour is usually large enough to contain a bench or chair and perhaps a table. An arbour can be used as a support for vines, but it may not have any plants growing on it — somewhat like a more open gazebo. The design of such arbours is important. The feeling or theme of the garden should be reflected in the design as well as in any furniture used in the arbour. An arbour that's little more than a covered "gateless gateway" provides a transition from one part of the garden to the other. Wrought-iron arbours are usually quite delicate and the plantings should be correspondingly light and airy to allow the design to be seen and appreciated.

Wood is commonly used in the construction of arbours, either in the form of planks, sheets of trellis material, or rustic poles. Galvanized nails and bolts should be used to connect the various parts. Uprights need to be embedded in concrete for stability and to prevent their heaving by frost.

Pergolas that have been successfully incorporated into the design have a purpose — they take the visitor or gardener somewhere or provide shelter. Ideally, a pergola should allow two or three people to walk side by side, but many suburban and urban gardens don't have the space to allow such a generous width. And don't forget that once the vines start to grow over it, the walkway will be smaller. With some clever planning and planting, however, a smaller-scale pergola can become a mysterious and enticing feature. A pergola of only one or two sections can act as a "doorway" from one section of the small garden to the other.

Wooden poles make a rustic pergola. Other materials that can be used for the uprights are wooden beams; brick, stone, or cement columns; metal or steel pipes or columns. The upright columns must be strong, for they will support not only the crossbeams but the weight of the vines that will grow on the crossbeams. Uprights should be well embedded in concrete so they can withstand strong winds.

The design of the pergola should be simple, just the uprights and crossbeams mentioned above. The main ornamental feature of the pergola is the planting it supports. (Look to arbours and gazebos for more decorative constructions.) A pergola looks best when smothered in vines. Good choices include one or a combination of the following: wisteria, grapes, clematis, climbing roses, honeysuckle, Virginia creeper, or silver lace vine, the latter a fast-growing dense climber that can get out of hand in three to five years. If you have room, plant vines that flower at different times — for example, a wisteria, which will flower in the spring,

Some uses for pergolas are:

- To divide one section of the garden from another
- To lead to different sections of the garden
- To provide a covered walkway
- To shelter a patio or deck
- To frame a view or garden feature, such as a beautiful bench or impressive plant specimen
- To make a welcoming front entrance

and an autumn-flowering clematis give two seasons of interest to the pergola. Don't overburden a delicate-looking pergola — even if the structure is well built, it may give the impression of imminent collapse.

A gazebo can be a focal point or a place from which to survey your garden. No matter how you intend to use the gazebo, keep its style true to the style of your garden — a copy of a Japanese tea house is appropriate for a serene Japanese garden, and an airy latticed structure will fit into a romantic English cottage or country garden. Gazebos are usually built of wood and painted or stained. The roof can be covered in a variety of ways — wooden shingles are attractive, but they should be in keeping with the style of the house and garden.

If the gazebo is to be used as a place of serenity and meditation, a place to read or relax, build in some comfortable benches or provide room for chairs or a small sofa. Some gazebos are open on all sides, others quite enclosed. Decide how protected from the elements you want to be, but ensure that when you're seated, you can see out of any openings or windows.

A great example of setting limits and enhancing the streetscape. There's a sense of commitment when you go through the arbour — this is a property you don't accidentally stray onto.

Another use for a gazebo is as a potting shed. It should be constructed so that from the outside none of the associated odds and ends are visible — all watering cans, pots, flats, bags of potting soil, seed packets, and so forth should be out of sight.

Decorations

I'm constantly amazed, surprised, and delighted by the array of garden decorations I come across in people's gardens. Whether they're expensive reproductions or unusual artefacts, I like what they tell me about the gardener. As a country of gardeners, we've moved beyond the traditional saintly figure, cherub, or mischievous young boy, although a place for them remains. Many gardeners still want to finish their garden with a piece of classic statuary. Some of the most common are figures in flowing robes, nymphs, cherubs, sea horses, and seashells. Other gardeners are attracted to the more whimsical, using figurines of animals such as cows, pigs, or lambs in a variety of materials, or pink flamingos.

The important thing is to carry the theme or style of garden through the decorations. Barnyard animals add a touch of the bucolic and look best in a country-style garden — one with flowing lines, colourful beds, and a cheerful atmosphere. If you have twig or rustic garden furniture, a flock of sheep — inanimate, of course! — grazing on the grass will look right at home. Gnomes and cartoon characters should be used sparingly. Placed strategically, flamingos can be used as a touch of humour in the garden. If you're making a statement — "This is a fun place to be!" — there's room for whimsical decorations in your garden. Otherwise, restraint is the key.

Statuary can provide a focal point — something the eye is drawn to immediately — or can be a pleasant surprise — a frog peeping out from beneath a group of hostas or a rabbit half-hidden by ferns. A romantic garden, full of rampant lush roses, intertwining clematis, and scented lavender, is the perfect spot for a cherub or nymph, but don't overdo it. One small statue is more impressive than three or four. Even in a small space, a figurine placed among containers can provide the finishing touch. However, statuary and garden design can make poor partners — be sure of the image you want to create before you purchase that piece you've just got to have.

Japanese-style gardens benefit from the careful placing of stone Japanese lanterns, Buddhas, miniature pagodas, or temple guard dogs. Wrought-iron sculptures can be particularly attractive in the winter. Not only do they stand out well against the snow, but their lines are emphasized by a dusting of snow. Decorative materials don't have to be freestanding. Bas-relief gargoyles, lions' heads, and sun faces are designed to be attached to walls or posts.

Sculpture and other works of art look best positioned with a hedge or wall as a backdrop. If the sculpture seems overwhelmed by surrounding growth, place it on a pedestal set among bushes to show it to advantage. Some sculpture is placed just around a corner or in a place where the garden visitor comes upon it as a pleasant surprise.

Benches, Chairs, Tables, and Umbrellas

The most important consideration when you're buying garden furniture is the purpose of the piece. Although it's possible to have furniture that's both comfortable and decorative, there's a great deal of attractive garden furniture that just isn't nice to sit in. Sit in the chair or on the bench before you buy it if you're looking for comfort. Get other family members to give it a try too. Is it easy to lower yourself into and get up from? Are there any bits that stick into tender parts of your body? Are the arms

Sundials and Gazing Globes

Sundials and gazing globes make nice focal points in the garden. Sundials need to be calibrated according to your particular location (for most people, a fussy undertaking involving knowing your latitude), so most commercially available ones are not really practical for time telling. But they make attractive garden decorations.

Gazing globes are made of mirrored glass and sit on pedestals. They look best situated among colourful flowers so they can reflect the lively colours. Don't place them near a play area, as they break easily, which is why I also recommend that you bring them indoors in a strong wind. Slightly irregular surfaces indicate that the globe has been hand-blown; moulded globes, which have seams, are less expensive. Floating a gazing globe or simple glass ball in a water garden will add a special dimension, and because of its mirrored appearance, a gazing globe makes a yard and garden appear larger than life.

Other Garden Decorations

The imagination knows no bounds when it comes to decorating and furnishing your garden. Here are some other possibilities to consider.

Birdbaths	Wall plaques	Tablecloths
Weather vanes	Decorative taps	Cushions
Name plates	Awnings	Wreaths

comfortable (and wide enough to hold a mug or book)? Can the back be adjusted? If the piece doesn't measure up on the comfort scale but you love it anyway, you may still want to buy it — as a piece of art. No matter how you use the furniture, it can always act as a focal point.

Whether your garden is a cottage garden, a formal garden, or more modern, there's a bench or chair to fill your need. All garden furniture should be able to withstand rain, and cushions should be waterproof or stored in a sheltered spot between uses. If you're short on storage space, look for furniture that can be folded, or choose materials that can be left outdoors all year round. Furniture that's left outside during rainstorms, snowfalls, and other inclement weather

This gazebo provides a nice little corner to get away from it all. Is there a gardener who doesn't have a yen for a gazebo?

requires some maintenance — washing, painting, rust removal — because of the wear and tear this weather causes. If you're going to leave furniture outside, buy pieces with brass or galvanized fasteners, which won't rust.

Twig furniture suits the rustic cottage garden; colourful chintz cushions can be added to make sitting more comfortable or to protect clothing. To extend the longevity of twig furniture, store it inside in the winter. Wicker and cane furniture, also at home in the cottage garden, are perennial

A single potted plant on one end of a bench makes a pretty effect.

A formal symmetrical bench is nicely set off by container plantings on each side. A twig bench or wicker seat looks best with a casual grouping of pots on the ground at one end.

favourites. Aluminum furniture that's a dead ringer for wicker is also available on the market and has the added advantage of being easy to clean. Painting any kind of furniture will help prolong its life and winter protection is desirable.

Wood blends in well with other garden furnishings and plantings and is comfortable to sit on. Many woods, especially cedar, weather well and require little maintenance, but softwoods such as pine need to be treated with a preservative annually. Seats should slope slightly or the seats should be slatted in some way to allow water to drain quickly. Most wooden furniture, especially if it's treated with preservatives, can be left out all year, giving some interest to the winter garden.

Wrought-iron and reproduction cast-iron furniture is suited to a romantic or formal garden. Depending on the design of the seat and back, wrought-iron chairs and benches may not always be comfortable, but they can look fabulous with a matching table. Padded chintz cushions not only make the chairs and benches more comfortable for sitting but also the lush floral patterns complement their usually ornate design and construction. Wrought iron demands some upkeep. Wash the furniture regularly and check for rusty spots every spring. When rust appears, or if paint has chipped, use a paint formulated for wrought iron to patch or repaint entirely. Store them in a protected place during the winter to prolong their life span, although you can leave them out without severe damage in the winter. They also look attractive in the winter garden, especially if they're painted in a colour that shows well against the snow.

For a garden that fulfils a number of functions — dining room, play room, relaxation area — moulded plastic resin, which never rusts, is the best choice. These chairs are usually stackable as well, so they're easy to put away for the winter. The designs are

Banners, Flags, Wind Socks, and Wind Chimes

Movement and sound are important elements in garden design. Both give pleasure, but as with other garden decorations, moderation and integration with your garden decor are important.

Fabric banners and flags add a cheerful note to a garden — or to any property, for that matter. People in many Scandinavian countries fly banners with their country's national colours to indicate that guests are visiting, which I think is a nice idea. You can fly a banner or flag all summer long to provide movement and interest in the garden, but the fabric should carry through the colour scheme of your plantings.

Wind socks are colourful fabric garden decorations that can be attached to a pole or hung from a balcony or window.

Japanese carp are often represented on these wind socks, but other figures are geese and ducks. In a breeze, the sock fills and moves; during still periods, it hangs limply. Don't leave them out over the winter — they're just a sad reminder of happy days in the garden.

Wind chimes are usually made of wood or metal but some "found" objects make good wind chimes, too. I recently saw some wind chimes made of old spoons and forks that had been flattened and curved as needed. I'm sure the sound they produced was not as melodious as those made of brass or bamboo, but they certainly were interesting looking! For good neighbourly relations, don't hang your wind chimes near the next-door neighbour's bedroom window.

A single piece of pottery can be a focal point. Its purpose is to attract attention — use it to deflect the eye away from a less than inspiring view or to jazz up the corner of a deck.

generally limited to a contemporary look, so they won't fit well into the English country or Japanese garden, for example.

Deck chairs, made of wood and canvas, add a relaxed holiday feel to a garden. The canvas may need to be replaced every few years, but many fabric shops sell striped or solid-colour canvas for replacements. Keep the wood in good repair and waterproof by painting it every year. Store in a dry place over the winter. In regions with heavy rainfalls, it's best to store deck chairs in a dry spot when they're not in use. Adirondack (also called Muskoka) chairs, made of wood, also give a cottagey, small-town feel to the garden and would be out of place in formal gardens. They often have wide arms, useful for drinks or putting down your

book while you wander off to do a bit of garden maintenance. Some people find the chairs difficult to get out of, as they're rather low to the ground; others see that as a good reason to stay put! Keep them painted or stained to protect from the weather and store in a dry place over the winter.

Benches are wonderful additions to small gardens, as their size will not make them seem out of place. A bench can be a wooden slab firmly attached to two sturdy uprights or a more elegant and impressive Lutyens-style bench. Set against a backdrop of an ivied wall, a Lutyens bench is a picture of perfection. These benches are made of wood and have rather high arms and a decorative back. Stone benches can be cold and hard to sit on, but in the right setting, especially a romantic garden, they'll be right at home. If benches are planned as part of a deck, they can be incorporated with planters. It's not difficult to make your own, if you're so inclined, or to purchase at a garden centre or hardware store.

Another type of bench is a wooden tree seat, which can be the answer to a barren spot under a tree. It can be a simple ring around the tree or designed to be more ornate with a decorative back. Leave enough space for the trunk to expand if the tree is not fully grown. The ground should be made level some distance out from the circular bench so that the sitter's feet can reach the ground. Don't put a tree seat under trees that drop sticky residues or that bear fruits that stain, such as mulberries.

Eating outdoors is one of the nicest things about summer. Food seems to taste better in the fresh air, and when it's been cooked on a nearby barbecue it's even better. However, tables can be used for purposes other than eating off. They can also be used as worktables for garden chores or as a place to display potted plants. Ornate iron legs topped with marble or other stone give a very different feel — of weight and solidity — from tables made of twig or wicker, which seem airy and light. Solid wood tabletops will not allow water to drain away quickly, so look for tables with slatted tops or small spaces between the lengths of wood. Wooden tables can be painted, stained, or left to weather naturally, though without some protective coating their life will be shorter. Because wooden tables can be heavy and cumbersome, plan on leaving them outdoors over the winter. If possible, move them to a sheltered area. You can cover them with a tarpaulin, though it's not very attractive to look at all winter, and high winds can tear off even the most carefully anchored cover. Tables with smooth or textured tempered glass are strong but heavy to move. Most transparent tabletops are made of acrylic, which is almost unbreakable, light, and easy to care for.

Umbrellas, which are available in many colours and patterns, add a cosmopolitan touch to the garden. They can be purchased free-standing, with a sturdy base, or as part of a table and chairs set. (Some manufacturers will even make umbrellas from material you supply.) The free-standing type of course offers more flexibility, as it can be moved around the garden to provide protection as needed. Keep umbrellas closed in windy weather, and hose them off with a strong jet of water every now and then to dislodge bits of leaves and twigs that can cause them to discolour. To prolong their life, store them in a dry place for the winter, although if space is at a premium, they can be left outdoors. Synthetic materials are usually inexpensive but will fade over the years. Canvas makes a beautiful, though expensive, umbrella that will need more care than the synthetic fabrics — at the beginning and end of the season, the fabric canopy should be scrubbed with a mild detergent specially formulated for fabrics. Rinse well after soaping, then leave open to dry. Canvas umbrellas should never be closed when they're wet or damp, as mildew will weaken the fibres.

Plant Containers

Containers can be decorative as well as providing a home for plants. Used alone or as an adjunct to beds, they provide the gardener with great versatility. Mix and match them to change colour schemes, to remove spent plants, and to provide a focal point in the garden.

Hammocks

Hammocks are a bit like canoes – you have to be careful getting in and out of them, but once you've got the technique perfected, you'll have a great time lying there gazing up at tree branches. Traditionally, hammocks are hung between two trees, but some hammocks come with their own frames so you can move them around. Whichever kind you choose, the hammock must be well supported. Don't attach a hammock to immature trees – both you and the trees could be damaged!

Hammocks are made of canvas, knotted rope, or synthetic material. If the material is a natural fibre, such as cotton, it will not stand being left outside in the winter. Even if your hammock is synthetic material, take it down in the fall. It doesn't add to the attractiveness of the winter garden.

Most flowerpots show off plants to best advantage when they don't compete with their colourful contents. Arranged in a group, potted plants can make a stunning display at the edge of a swimming pool, at the corner of a deck, or marching up steps, and can be rearranged to provide different colour and plant combinations. Hanging baskets with romantic airy plantings enhance the gingerbread decorative work on a turn-of-the-century porch. Wire half baskets full of ferns and impatiens can brighten shady side gardens when they're attached to a fence or the wall of the house.

Although many houses don't have window sills to which window boxes can be attached, many of us have a great fondness for the way they look. It's not surprising, then, that manufacturers have met that need with hardware to firmly attach boxes to window areas — either directly to a house, a window frame, or even a railing. If they are attached to a window, easy access is needed for watering, deadheading, and fertilizing. Window boxes need to be positioned carefully — water can sometimes leak out of the drainage holes, staining whatever is beneath them. In spite of what may sound like a lot of drawbacks, many people go to great lengths to install window boxes for the attractive European feeling they give.

It's easy to find flowerpots in attractive shapes and designs that fit in with the theme of your garden. Crisp, clean shapes look best with a modern or even classical formal style, and more ornate pots are shown off to best advantage in a romantic garden. Rustic finishes or designs are appropriate for a cottage garden. One stunning specimen plant in a simple elegant container situated at the end of a path, around a corner, or at the entrance to the house can transform an ordinary scene into one of beauty.

Objects that can be used as planters are almost limitless. If it can hold soil, it's a planter, as long as it has good drainage. Tubs, half barrels, baskets, sinks, and troughs are only a few of the containers you can use. As with other garden accessories, though, match the type of container to the mood or theme of your garden. Urns are rather formal, although the type of design and pattern can make them appropriate for gardens with a more casual mood. They also often have decorative handles, which make them attractive on their own, appropriate for an unplanted display. You may even want to place the urn on its own pedestal.

Containers are constructed from many materials — wood, metal, fibreglass, terra cotta, and ceramic are common. Planters made from redwood or cedar are rot resistant, although lining any wooden planter with a plastic liner (which can be made from a garbage bag) will extend its life.

Another type of container is the jardiniere. This is usually a decorative ceramic or stoneware jar used to display houseplants or other plants. The potted plant is set in the jardiniere, sometimes on a bed of pebbles to allow excess water to drain away and to prevent the plant from sitting in water. Jardinieres are available from garden centres and some housewares stores in an assortment of shapes, sizes, and colours.

In a cottage garden, consider adding a few strawberry pots — tall cylindrical-shaped red clay pots with little openings into which small plants can be put. The top is open and can be planted as well. In spite

of their name, plants other than strawberries can be grown in them. Drought-tolerant herbs and sedums do especially well, as the soil tends to dry out quickly.

This grand view calls for elegant seating — a stately perch from which to take in the gorgeous landscapes.

Fountains

A small decorative fountain can make a great difference to the look and sound of your garden. The eye is drawn to water, especially when the water is moving. If you already have a water garden, you know how hypnotic and calming water, whether still or running, is.

Adding a fountain to a garden is simple, as long as there is an outdoor electrical supply nearby. If you're adding an electrical outlet to the garden, hire a licensed electrician to do the job (and make it one of the jobs that gets done in Year 1). Water and electricity are a potent and potentially fatal mix — you do not want to take chances. Specify that a circuit breaker is to be installed for safety's sake.

Fountains can be free-standing or submerged in a water garden, be part of a garden feature such as a rock or millstone from which the water issues, or be part of a figurine or piece of statuary from which water flows into the water garden or other receptacle. Sometimes these pieces of statuary are mounted on a wall or fence. The free-standing fountain and its pump should sit on a stable base and be easily accessible so that the filter can be cleaned. Pumps can be either submersible or surface, but the former is most appropriate for home use. Submersible pumps are very quiet and are becoming more inexpensive all the time. Surface pumps are used when a great volume of water needs to be circulated, such as in a large pond.

Fountainheads throw out various water patterns, depending on their design — everything from a continuous, steady stream to a misty trickle. When you're purchasing equipment for the fountain, make sure your pump is powerful enough to produce the flow you need. Most home gardens are best served by fairly simple fountains, or their effect becomes overwhelming rather than relaxing. Incorporating a free-standing fountain in a formal or symmetrical design will look better than using one in a more "natural" design of irregular shapes.

Some fountains are composed simply of the nozzle throwing up its pattern of water, but others are figures or statues holding jugs, bottles, or fish from which the water pours into the pool. Once again, your choice should reflect the theme of your garden.

Another type of free-standing fountain, sometimes called a bubble fountain, is one that is not part of a water garden but is incorporated into a millstone or rock. Such a fountain makes a wonderful focal point. The water bubbles out of an opening in the rock or centre of the millstone, spilling over it to a bed of river rock. The whole thing is set in a concealed reservoir, where the pump is housed, recirculating the water. Sometimes the feature is just a bed of river rock or attractive pebbles, without the millstone, but the principle is the same.

Wall fountains, or water spouts, are perfect for a small garden. They don't take up much space and are easy to dismantle for the winter. The range of such fountains is almost endless — a sculpture, mask, gargoyle, lion's head, sun face, and so forth. Found objects can sometimes be fashioned into a wall fountain, with a little imagination and ingenuity. Through an opening in the ornament, the water will trickle into a basin or other receptacle and be pumped back up to be recirculated. They're quite easy to put together — besides your ornament and a small recirculating pump, you just need an

Whether moving or still, water adds life and interest to a garden. Moving, it masks ambient noise and creates a constantly changing picture. Still, it mirrors the sky and clouds.

electrical supply and a strong wall to attach the object to. Attach the ornament securely to the wall; below the ornament place the water receptacle, which should be deep enough that the small pump can be immersed. The tubing that takes the water from the pump to the outlet in the ornament can snake behind the wall or be guided up the wall (and hidden with foliage). Fill the basin with water, plug in the pump, and you've got an instant bit of paradise.

Lighting

Summer is all too short in our country, and I for one want to get as much use out of my garden as I can. Installing lighting is a great way to extend the hours you spend socializing and relaxing on your deck or patio or by the pool. Temporary lighting that's provided by candles, lamps, flares, and torches can whet your appetite for more permanent installations.

You don't have to spend a fortune on lighting to get what you want — but if you do, it's well worth the money. When the sun goes down and your outdoor lights come on, you'll see that your yard takes on a new character. It's like living with two gardens — a daytime garden and a nighttime one. As with other elements of the garden, though, don't overdo it. The idea is not to recreate the daylight but to add a new dimension to the garden and increase your

Lighting performs several functions in the garden: it enhances safety and security; and it can be used to highlight attractive features.

enjoyment. A well-directed spotlight will have greater impact than a flood-light lighting the whole garden.

Accent lights — low-voltage fixtures — are used along walkways. They usually have a cap and louvres that are adjustable or removable so you can direct the light where you want it. They are easy to install and available in many garden centres and hardware stores. Post lights and garden lights are taller than accent lights, but they too have adjustable louvres. They throw out a wider beam of light and are used for pathways or in flowerbeds.

The transformer that plugs into the outlet sometimes contains a timer so your lights turn on and off at a particular time. Or you can purchase solar lights with a switch activated by the setting and rising of the sun.

Floodlights are used to light a particular feature, create a mood, or provide security lighting. Some have a variable focus ring to help customize the light you want. Others feature a motion detector so that they come on only when they sense movement — they may be smart, but they're not smart enough to distinguish between nighttime prowlers such as cats and raccoons and the human variety who may not be so innocent.

Here are some tips to keep in mind when you're adding lighting to your garden design.

🦋 Be judicious in your use of coloured lights in the garden. Red and green lights may be fine at Christmas, but as a permanent feature of the garden, they may grow tiresome.

🦋 Avoid aiming a floodlight into an area where you will be sitting, and be sure to avoid lighting your neighbours' yards — they probably want privacy, too!

🦋 Lights used to illuminate a path should be above or below eye level to avoid blinding people who are walking.

🦋 Use garden plantings and structures to conceal the lighting fixtures, unless the fixtures themselves are ornamental.

🦋 When lighting statuary, an interesting wall, or a particular plant, use a small spotlight to direct the light at the object. Experiment to get the best play of light and shadow.

🦋 Use lighting to emphasize shrubs and trees with interesting leaves and branches, such as the corkscrew hazel.

🦋 A light that shines down through branches and leaves gives a dappled effect.

🦋 For a dramatic effect, light plants from below rather than from above.

🦋 In the winter, light stark tree or shrub branches to cast shadows on the snow for a spectacular effect. In a snowfall, the light will catch the falling flakes, creating a constantly changing garden feature.

🦋 Use a spotlight to highlight a particular plant growing in or over a water garden.

🦋 An underwater light adds mystery and excitement to a water garden, especially if it catches the glint of goldfish moving in the water. And don't forget the swimming pool — it can look extraordinarily beautiful when lighted at night from underwater.

● Light a fountain so that the light goes through the jet of water, creating sparkling jewels of water.

Set a candle in the lantern for a soft glow on a summer's evening.

Swimming Pools and Hot Tubs

Deciding to take the plunge — pun intended! — and put in a swimming pool opens up new gardening and outdoor decorating challenges. The main challenge is to incorporate features such as pools and hot tubs into the general landscape so that they're inviting and yet don't overwhelm.

● If you have children, situate the pool or tub so it's easily seen from the house. However, you'll be looking at the covered pool all winter long, so if views are

Summertime and the living is easy — comfy deck chairs, a sturdy attractive table, and some container plants to make it pretty. Reach out and pick a fresh tomato — what could be better?

important to you and safety is not an issue, screen it with a trellis, trees, a wall, or a hedge.

🌿 Pool interiors are available in a range of colours nowadays. A dark blue-grey pool interior will reflect light nicely, making a lovely mirrorlike surface. Co-ordinate the colour of interior with the material that will be used as decking or paving around the pool. This colour scheme can be carried through into the patio furniture, umbrellas, and the containers for potted plants.

🌿 Even a small area can house a pool. A lap pool is a long narrow pool, usually of a uniform depth, used mainly for exercising. Above-ground pools are

affordable alternatives, especially if you have a sloping site. You can have fun designing a deck and plantings to make it look like an inground pool.

🌿 If you're installing an inground pool, use the excavated soil to build up areas of the garden or a rock garden. Don't plunk these raised areas — sometimes called berms — just anywhere, though. They should look as if they naturally belong in your landscape.

🌿 Have fun with the method you choose to house the pool equipment — the pump and filter. Perhaps a changing room could be part of the building the equipment is housed in. Remember that the pump makes a noise so you don't want it too close to the main seating area.

🌿 Container plantings really come into their own around the pool or hot tub. A few words of caution, though: don't place them where they're in the way of people who are getting into and out of the water; don't put them too close to the water's edge as chemicals used in the pool can damage or even kill them and leaves dropping into the pool will be a nuisance. Avoid plants that attract bees and other stinging insects and those that produce berries that can stain a deck or pavement.

🍃 Many municipalities require that pools be fenced for safety and this can some-times make it hard to incorporate the pool into a pleasingly designed land-scape. Check with your municipality to see if there are bylaws against planting shrubs or vines to disguise the chain-link fence that seems to be the fence of choice around pools.

🍃 Allow room in your design for safety equipment, such as a rescue pole or flotation devices, to be kept near the pool.

🍃 Incorporate arbours and pergolas into the design for your hot tub location. Or use awnings to provide overhead pro-tection when you want it.

🍃 Situate the hot tub so it's easily accessi-ble from the house. Even in our cold Canadian climate, a dip in the hot tub on a cold winter's day is not unusual — I do it all the time (it's fun watching the snow fall while sitting in the hot tub).

🍃 If you're unlikely to use the hot tub in the winter, you have more flexibility in where you site it. If it's a place of relax-ation you want, put the tub where you can't hear the phone or doorbell. Sur-round it with masses of luxurious

potted plants or lattice on which you can grow vines.

🍃 Maintain a view but protect the tub from prevailing winds with clear acrylic sheets made into "walls." This is an especially good idea for locations that overlook a sea view, where the winds can be strong, or on a hillside with a fabulous view.

🍃 You'll find a hot tub more enjoyable to use if it's placed where it gives a view of the garden but is itself situated in a pri-vate spot.

An important consideration for the pool or hot tub area is the material used to sur-round it and provide the walking and sit-ting area. The decking around the pool or hot tub should be a non-slip material and able to withstand the extremes of tempera-ture and weather conditions. New products on the market provide durability with easy care — one such is a type of wood made from waste wood products. It fades to a pleasant soft grey, and although it can be painted, it can be left as is year after year with no rotting and no slivers! Redwood is expensive but resists rot and is therefore long lasting as a natural wood decking material. If unpainted, it will weather to an appealing brown-grey. Cedar is strong, lightweight, rot resistant, and less expensive than redwood. It weathers to a silver grey if not treated with a sealer. You can apply skid-resistant plastic or polymer coatings, available in a variety of colours, to plywood decking.

Areas for Play, Work, and Composting

Kids' Play Areas

The joy many of us take from our gardens is increased greatly by seeing our children, grandchildren, nieces, nephews, and friends' and neighbours' kids playing in our yard. We want to make it a friendly and safe place for them. Of course, sometimes their idea of a great yard and your idea can differ. A kid may see your pride-of-joy perennial bed as the wall of a castle or a wonderful place to hide from invaders from outer space. However, with planning, you can accommodate your child's play needs with your desire to grow things, and you can plan for the future as your child outgrows sandboxes and swing sets.

If you are fortunate enough to have a large space, of course, you'll find it easy to accommodate a play area for your kids. But families with smaller spaces will need to be a bit more ingenious in how they use their space.

Safety is the most important issue when it comes to children's play areas and equipment. Be sure the area is visible from the house. Children like space to run around in, so try to incorporate some running space. However, this may not be possible in very small gardens, and a sandbox or swing set may well be a better use of space.

If possible, build or buy playground equipment that can be adjusted as the children grow. The ground cover is an important consideration, as well. Sand, pea gravel, or small or shredded wood chips to a depth of at least 15 cm (6 inches) will soften the impact of a fall. Grass is soft too, but it can get worn down quickly, and the ground beneath it can become concrete hard in a

short time. The ground cover should extend out from the play area for about 1.8 m (6 feet) in all directions.

It's best to designate a section of the garden as the play area so it's clear what's off limits. If the children also have a place where they can nurture some of their own special plants, such as sunflowers or scarlet runner beans, they'll learn to respect the plantings of others. If you haven't got the space to do this and want to give the entire garden over to the children, fulfil your gardening needs by planting in containers or

A well-designed work area adds an elegant touch to the garden.

....

putting all your energy into the front yard. The years we have with our small children are really very short, and the time to garden when they've grown is quite long.

Swings and sandboxes are the mainstays of any play area. These two simple pieces of play equipment can provide kids with many happy hours. Provide your sandbox with a cover that's put on when the box

isn't in use to keep out cats and other animals. When the sandbox has outgrown its usefulness, turn it into a flowerbed or water garden. A hammock makes a nice change from a swing. It's a good getaway for the child who wants a little time on his or her own with a book or to share with a friend for some chatter. Hammocks for children should be well constructed, with a rod at each end to keep the mesh fairly flat and open.

A climbing frame is a space-efficient piece of play equipment that will get a lot of

use. A climbing frame can be incorporated with other pieces such as slides, swings, and platforms, and even an outdoor toybox. Children are generally happier with toys and play equipment that can be adapted for many uses, so it's often better to go for the simple design rather than the elaborate.

Kids love tree houses — they're great places to get away from parents. A tree house doesn't have to be elaborate: a good sturdy platform with equally sturdy walls and a ladder will do. Not all trees are suitable to have house built in them. There must be a horizontal plane on which the platform can be built. If you have two strong trees growing fairly closely together, the tree house could span the two trees. As well, a tree house can be built on well-grounded stilts, either with the tree coming up the middle of the platform or to one side of the platform. Access to tree houses is provided by a ladder (preferably not hammered to the tree) or a rope ladder that can be pulled up after the last person is in.

Kids' play equipment doesn't have to be elaborate for them to have hours of enjoyment. It'll be years before my son tires of this simple swing.

Be careful how you attach the structure to the tree. Lashing the tree house to the tree with cable can cause damage to the tree. Nails are fine, especially if the tree house will not be a permanent addition to your garden. If you want it to stay put for more than four or five years, large screws can be used.

If you have the space, have fun incorporating a playhouse into your design. They range from the simple — four walls, a roof, a window, and door — to the elaborate — secret passages, lookout towers, built-in chests for storage. If you're designing your own, keep the future in mind; will you be able to adapt it to your own uses when the children have grown up? — as a storage shed, for example.

The best play spaces include objects that can be adapted for many uses.

Work and Compost Areas

For the putterer, there's nothing better than a small shed or separate area with a worktable to mess about with cuttings, seeds, and so on. It can be hard to rein in one's enthusiasm when dreaming of the perfect potting shed or storage shed, so go ahead and make your wish list — shelves, hooks, electricity, running water, lots of room for bags of fertilizer and grass seed, more work space than seems necessary. . .Need I go on? You've probably got your own special list by now. It's all too likely that you'll have to scale down your dreams, but you can probably claim a few yards or metres to make a small work area. At the very least, such a spot will provide some shelter so you can work even in a light drizzle, but ideally the work area should be enclosed on all sides and have a roof, so it can double as a storage area. If you have the room, some very charming sheds can be built following simple plans or bought ready-made.

I can't imagine a garden without a composter, either purchased or homemade. The ideal spot is one that's protected from strong winds, on level ground that drains well, in the sun if it's a commercial composter, and away from eavestroughs and downspouts.

Barbecue Area

I talked earlier about the pleasures of eating outdoors, and cooking outdoors is every bit as enjoyable. Many Canadians eagerly look forward to the first barbecue of the season — in fact, some hardy souls barbecue during the winter on a regular basis. Your barbecue equipment may be no more than a hibachi, but where you situate it is still a part of your design.

The barbecue area should be close to the house. You'll use it more often if it's easy to get to. Also, in inclement weather, you can move things into the house more quickly. Being close to the house gives you access to electrical outlets needed for a spit, lighting, or plugging in appliances.

Try to situate the barbecue so it's protected from the prevailing wind and not near windows or door — yours or the neighbours'. Barbecuing causes a lot of smoke that's best left outside. Keep the barbecue away from walls of buildings and from trees and shrubs. The intense heat can cause paint to blister, plastic to buckle, and greenery to become damaged or even catch fire.

Purchased barbecues have the advantage of portability. The barbecue can be tucked out of sight in a garage or shed, or you can construct an area to keep it out of sight — perhaps behind a short latticed wall or a "wall" of container plants. Herbs planted nearby, either in their own bed or in containers, not only add interest but can be used in the cooking.

Highly scented plants that attract bees, wasps, and other stinging insects should not be planted too near the barbecue area. The smell of cooking food will attract some insects, but by planting insect-attracting plants away from the area, you'll help to lessen their numbers.

Personalizing your garden with furnishings is a process — probably one that is in constant forward motion. So take your time and enjoy reflecting on your own personal stories associated with the items in your garden. Relax and reflect on these treasures — relaxation and reflection are the two greatest gifts any garden can give to the gardener.

5

The Plants

Up until now, your sketches have been pretty general, taking into account your local conditions, your family's needs, and your ideas about colour, shapes, and textures. Now it's time to start adding some detail in the form of plants.

Now we come to the "building blocks" of the garden: the plants. At first, the choices of plants may seem overwhelming. Just walking down the aisles of your local garden centre can send you home reeling in indecision — or loaded down with a hodge podge. That's where your plan comes in. Up until now, your sketches have been pretty general, taking into account your local conditions, your family's needs, and your ideas about colour, shapes, and textures. Now it's time to start adding some detail in the form of plants. As you choose the plants (the lists that follow will help you get started), keep in mind the concepts of colour, texture, and shape that I've already discussed — and the plants' ultimate size. All these elements will play their role in making your garden visually pleasing. As well, it's easy to get distracted from your purpose as you leaf through catalogues and encyclopedias of plants and browse at the garden centre. If you've gone to the trouble of doing the planning preparations I've outlined, this is not the time to get waylaid. Many of us are attracted to a particular type of plant over and over — we love delicate blue flowers and fill our gardens with flax and lobelia and blue asters, or it's big bold foliage that attracts us and we go for hostas and bergenia. Of course there's nothing wrong with growing exactly what you want, but if you're aiming for a well-designed garden, you'll want some variety. Just as it's the spice of life, so will it add zing and flavour to your yard.

On the ground, up the wall, in containers — a great example of not wasting a bit of planting space. In addition, many seasons of interest have been planned for by using euonymus.

Few of us start with a clean slate, so to speak, as we design our gardens and choose the plants we'll fill them with. Often we've inherited a previous owner's plants, or in the case of a garden renovation it's our own fancies of previous years we have to make some hard decisions about. What will go and what will stay? What can be moved? Once that's been decided, assess the conditions your plants will be growing in, as outlined in Chapter 1. Review what you want the plants to do: hide a view, act as a focal point, carry out a colour scheme, convey a particular feeling. As you move through this process, you'll be

A perfect setting for the home — a healthy lawn with attention paid to the edgings. The final touch is Mother Nature's intricate shadows on the grass.

narrowing the choices of plants available — but never fear, you'll still have a vast array to choose from.

Later in the book, I'll talk about different types of gardens and suggest some plantings for them, but here I want to talk a bit more generally about plants and their part in the garden design. One basic and sometimes controversial element is the lawn.

Established plants that should be removed are those that do not fit your long-term plans. However, exceptional mature plants are worth keeping.

Grass and the Lawn

I like grass and can't imagine a yard without some area of lawn. But many people are getting rid of their lawns and replacing them with patios, decks, ground covers, or flowerbeds. One of the questions I suggested you ask yourself in Chapter 1 was whether you wanted a lawn, and you may have decided by now that it will be a feature of your garden. Lawns offer a soothing expanse to set off the more vibrant colours of spring bulbs, summer annuals and perennials, and brilliant fall leaves and make an attractive contrast to the textures of paths, decks, and paving.

From a design perspective, the lawn should be an integral part of the garden plan, rather than the space that's left over after everything else has been plotted out. A lawn can help to tie together the various elements of the design, as its colour and uniform texture bring unity and cohesion to the plan. If upkeep is an issue in your household, you can make lawn-mowing an easier chore by designing the edges of the lawn (which of course are often the edges of the flowerbeds) to be softly curving or straight — the more complicated the shape of the lawn, the more difficult it will be to mow. Setting specimen shrubs or small trees into

the lawn will also increase mowing time as you have to mow around them. If easy mowing is important to you, group trees and shrubs together so that they're in one large bed rather than several small beds. Don't let the grass grow close to the trunk, but extend the bed well away from branches. The exposed earth can be covered with attractive mulches such as wood chippings or shredded bark.

If you're a lawn lover, you'll be facing two choices: to renovate your existing lawn, or sow grass seed or lay sod on a bare area you want to turn into a lawn. If you're doing an extensive redesign of an existing garden, starting all over with the lawn, and seeding or sodding it, may be the wisest route, since the lawn will come in for some intensive use if heavy equipment is being brought in — to construct a swimming pool, for example — of if workers are tramping back and forth as they build a shed or gazebo. But if your design doesn't call for major work, or if you are implementing the design in stages, don't give up on the grass too quickly. Some special care — keeping it well watered, cutting it not too short, and fertilizing on a regular basis — will soon pay off. For more information about lawn care, check out my books *A Greener Thumb* and *The All Seasons Gardener*.

> A lawn that slopes away from the house gives the impression that it's larger than it really is.

Soil: The pH Scale

A feature of soil that will affect your plants is its acidity or alkalinity, the range from one to the other called the pH scale. Most plants listed in this book grow well in soil with a pH in the neutral range, from 6 to 8, unless otherwise noted. The higher numbers represent alkaline soil; the lower represent acid soil. You can purchase kits at garden centres to measure the pH in your soil or send a soil sample to a provincial Department of Agriculture. Digging in lots of well-rotted compost will help balance an excessively alkaline or acid soil and thus give you more flexibility in your plant choices.

Use creeping and sprawling plants such as woolly thyme or Irish moss to soften the edges of paths or grow between stones.

Ground Covers

Ground covers make good alternatives to lawns and paved areas and can be used in place of them or in addition to them. They're often the solution for hard-to-mow slopes, although initially they'll still need weeding, and some plants will need cutting back now and then — there's no such thing as the maintenance-free garden, just low maintenance.

Ground covers can be chosen for all kinds of aesthetic reasons — for their colours to complement other plantings, to provide texture or shape contrasts, to act as a bridge between colour schemes. They can also be chosen for practical reasons — on a slope, as I mentioned above, in a shady area where little else will grow, or to keep maintenance to a minimum. Ground covers can also make a bold statement: try a mass planting of pachysandra as a simple transition from one part of a shady garden to another or merely to cut down on the amount of lawn. In addition, they will make a lovely contrast to the lawn — their texture is different, as is their colour.

Here are some perennial ground covers for particular conditions or uses — there are many other general-purpose ground covers, but I've picked some for special situations. You'll find more ground covers in the listings for perennials and annuals on pages 133 to 140. As well, many of the plants in the section on vines and climbers can be used as ground covers — there's no rule that says they must grow up a wall, trellis, pergola, or other structure. Unfortunately, though, most ground covers are not appropriate for areas where there is heavy foot traffic — for those areas, grass is best.

- Barrenwort (*Epimedium*): Plant in sun or partial shade in well-drained humus-rich soil. Its green elongated pointy leaves turns a dry reddish brown in winter. Small sprays of flowers in pink, white, violet, or yellow appear from mid-spring to early summer. It makes a good contrast to ferns and hostas. Height: 22 cm (9 inches). Zone 3.

- Bearberry (*Arctostaphylos uva-ursi*): Plant bearberry in a sunny spot in sandy acid soil. It's good on banks and is particularly suited to seaside and mountain conditions. Its bright green leaves will make a glossy mat, but until it's established,

mulch between plants. Its pink flowers are touched with white and are followed by red fruit in late spring. Height: 15 to 30 cm (6 to 12 inches). Zone 2.

🌺 Bergenia (*Bergenia*): Bergenias will tolerate full sun only if they have some afternoon shade; otherwise, plant in a shady area. Give them fertile humus-rich soil. Their lustrous, leathery foliage, which looks good with ferns, hostas, rhododendrons, and hellebores, provides a nice texture. In addition, the leaves stay green in the winter except in extreme cold. Small white or pink clusters of

This lawn becomes a kind of path through the garden. The finely clipped hedge marks the transition from the more formal part of the garden to the more casual area.

flowers bloom in the spring. Height: 45 to 60 cm (18 to 24 inches). Zone 3.

🌺 Bloodroot (*Sanguinaria canadensis*): A must for those who love native flowers, bloodroot blooms in early spring with yellow-centred white flowers; during the rest of the season, its flat lobed leaves cover the ground. It does best in moist rich soil. Grow it in partial shade.

Height: 10 to 22 cm (4 to 9 inches). Zone 3.

🌺 Creeping Jenny (*Lysimachia nummularia*): Boggy areas are a natural habitat for this low-growing plant. Full shade will produce lush growth and long trailing stems that can become invasive, but a drier sunnier situation gives denser growth. Small cup-shaped yellow flowers, which bloom in the summer, and round leaves make an attractive contrast to plants with long thin leaves. Height: 15 cm (6 inches). Zone 3.

🌺 Creeping juniper (*Juniperus horizontalis*): The evergreen creeping juniper will make a shallow dense carpet and has green, blue-green or silvery needles. It likes the sun but will tolerate a wide range of conditions; it's available in many varieties. Height: 10 to 45 cm (4 to 18 inches). Zone 3.

🌺 Euonymus (*Euonymus*): This useful plant tolerates many conditions from fairly deep shade to full sun. Some varieties are evergreen, some deciduous. The leaves are usually shiny dark green, though there are some variegated types available as well. Euonymus can be left to ramble unchecked, but it also lends itself to clipping — in all, a very versatile plant. Height: depends on variety. Zone 3, but check variety.

🌺 Heather (*Erica*): Heathers will grow in light shade to full sun. Foliage is dark green, grey-green, or bronzy green in summer, bronzy red in winter, depending on the variety. Their tiny blooms are pink, red, purple, or white. The foliage and shape of heather contrasts nicely with rhododendrons, both of which need acid soil. Height: depends on variety, but usually about 30 cm (1

Ground Covers for Special Situations

Slopes: bearberry, creeping juniper, wild ginger, crown vetch.

Rocky slopes: barrenwort, euonymus (look for 'San Jose', 'Wilton Carpet', 'Andorra compacta'), sedums, three-toothed cinquefoil, foamflower.

Under Trees: barrenwort, pachysandra, junipers, foamflower, wild ginger, barren strawberry, bloodroot, wood sorrel.

Dry Conditions: three-toothed cinquefoil, sedum.

Sandy Soil: bearberry, creeping juniper, sedum.

Acid Soil: bearberry, heather, bluebead lily, three-toothed cinquefoil, wintergreen, Canada mayflower, bunchberry, periwinkle.

Alkaline Soil: clematis, Virginia creeper.

Moist Soil: creeping Jenny, wintergreen, mayapple, Christmas fern, cinnamon fern, Japanese painted fern.

Shade: barrenwort, bergenia, creeping Jenny, euonymus, pachysandra, periwinkle, Virginia creeper, wintergreen, wild ginger, foamflower, mayapple, violets, bloodroot, ajuga.

Sun: barrenwort, creeping Jenny, euonymus, sedums, Virginia creeper, wild strawberry, bearberry, creeping juniper, heather, three-toothed cinquefoil.

Winter Interest: junipers, euonymus, bergenia.

foot). Zone 5, but check — some are more tender.

🌱 Pachysandra (*Pachysandra terminalis*): The sheltered shade of trees gives pachysandra ideal conditions, though in very dry weather you'll need to water it. Its glossy leaves are evergreen and will turn yellow if exposed to too much sun. Although it produces tiny white flowers in late spring, it's grown for its foliage. Height: 30 cm (1 foot). Zone 3.

Even in early spring, these ground covers are at work. They help keep weeds down and hide the foliage of bulbs that have finished blooming.

🌱 Periwinkle (*Vinca minor*): This trailing plant with glossy evergreen leaves and purple starry flowers withstands pollution, so it will not suffer if planted near streets. It prefers moist soil and light shade but will grow fairly slowly in deep shade. Height: 5 to 10 cm (2 to 4 inches). Zone 4.

- Sedum (*Sedum*): A large group of tough, low-maintenance, drought-tolerant plants that love the sun and are happy in poor soil. Goldmoss sedum will form flat dense mats and produce yellow flowers in the summer. It's quite a rampant grower and can eventually get out of hand, so it's best not to try to combine it too closely with other plants. Height: Varies, but most are under 30 cm (12 inches). Zone 2.

- Three-toothed cinquefoil (*Potentilla tridentata*): Plant this creeper in full sun in dry acid soil. Its fan-shaped deep green leaves stay attractive during the spring and summer, then turn dark red in the fall before dropping. Small white flowers similar to those of strawberries bloom in early summer. Height: 30 cm (12 inches). Zone 2.

- Virginia creeper (*Parthenocissus quinquefolia*): A versatile vine that can be used as a ground cover, it grow in full shade or full sun. In the fall, its green foliage turns bright red and the small white or green flowers turn into blue-black berries. It looks especially good in the fall against dark walls — it will seem to shine. It's a good plant for urban areas because it tolerates pollution. Height: 22 cm (9 inches). Zone 2.

- Wild ginger (*Asarum canadense*): The woodland garden, with its shade and moist, rich soil, is the perfect place for wild ginger. Its large matte heart-shaped leaves contrast prettily with the foliage of ferns. Once established, wild ginger spreads rapidly. Height: 20 cm (8 inches). Zone 3.

- Wintergreen (*Gaultheria procumbens*): Wintergreen does best in acid soil that's on the moist side and in the shade, although it will tolerate sun. Its evergreen dark green leaves turn red in the cold; the pink-white flowers bloom all summer and are followed by red fruit that stays throughout winter. Height: 15 cm (6 inches). Zone 3.

Trees for Special Situations

The evergreens provide winter interest because of their foliage and shape, but don't overlook the beauty of bare branches against snow or silhouetted against a clear blue winter sky. It can be hard to imagine what that little tree will be like as it matures and how it will change your landscape, winter and summer. If being able to see the tree from the house in winter is important to you, make sure you've taken the mature spread into account when you plant it. As it grows, it should be a sufficient distance away from the house so that viewing it is possible, rather than having it covering a window!

Shade trees (that is, the trees provide shade): ash (white, green), beech, birch (white, grey, weeping), catalpa (northern), chestnut, little leaf linden, locust ('Shademaker', 'Skyline', 'Sunburst'), maple (Norway, sugar, soft), mountain ash, oak (red, white, pin), walnut (black, English).

Dwarf trees: flowering almond, weeping caragana, catalpa ('Mophead'), crabapple, Japanese maple.

Evergreen trees: fir (silver, Fraser, Douglas), Canadian hemlock, Austrian pine, spruce (Norway, Serbian, white).

Trees

Trees play an important part in the garden design, since they're such large and dramatic features. Trees add the element of height; they also provide the "ceiling" or roof to your garden room. As with lawns, you're likely to be dealing with trees that already exist in your garden. A significantly large tree will dictate where flowerbeds and water gardens go, what will grow in the beds, where it's pleasant to sit, where grass will grow, and so on. Don't give in to an immediate impulse to get rid of a tree. Some judicious pruning can turn an overgrown shabby-looking tree into a thing of beauty. In addition, some municipalities have stringent bylaws regarding the cutting down of trees,

Trees give a sense of permanence. Assess the condition of existing trees if you're renovating your garden. Sometimes a good pruning is all that's needed to restore a tree to its natural beauty.

so check carefully. If cutting down the tree seems to be the only answer, do yourself — and the plant — one last favour. Check out how the absence of the tree will affect the view. It might have been planted there for a purpose. The problem might not be the tree but what's growing, or not growing, around it. If you decide on a reprieve for a large tree, it can still be challenging to accommodate your plans to it, but here are a few ideas.

Incorporate seating around the base of the tree. A beautiful wooden bench that encircles the trunk looks inviting. It's a cool place to sit, and a few containers with shade-loving plants add to the scene. The ground should be level so it's comfortable for sitting.

Cultivate the ground around the tree and plant spring-flowering bulbs, to be replaced with shade-loving annuals or perennials as the foliage dies down.

A flowering magnolia makes a lovely focal point in the spring garden. It's best to situate it where it will shine when blooming but will fade into the background the rest of the year.

Some trees with shallow roots, such as maples, seem to defeat us, no matter what we do. Two solutions: first, set attractive containers around the base of the tree, and fill them with annuals such as impatiens, begonias, and lobelia for a fabulous sight; or second, build shallow raised beds around the tree, and plant

If you're looking for a vertical accent in the garden, consider some of the narrow, tall evergreens. They'll look good all year round, and most are not fussy about their growing conditions.

with annuals and perennials that like the shade — hostas and ferns make lovely companions with their contrasting textures, shapes, and colours.

If you're facing a new garden, perhaps in a new subdivision, a mature tree will make a great difference, especially on a small lot. It may take a few years to reach its mature height, but you'll have the satisfaction of seeing it grow and bring your plan to life. The shade it provides will shelter you and your house, and as I mentioned above, it will introduce an element of height to your plan, something that's easy to forget if you've done only bird's-eye-view sketches.

I've assembled a list of trees and shrubs with notes of the conditions they like and any special features that will help you incorporate them into your landscape —I've also described a few my favourites. As with all these lists, there are hundreds of others to choose from — consider this an introductory list. Here are a few things to keep in mind as you narrow down your choices:

- The mature height and spread of the tree;

- The flowering period, if any;

- The hardiness of the tree;

- The purpose of the tree in your design;

- Whether the tree is evergreen or deciduous.

- Ash (*Fraxinus*): What a wonderful tree! It stands up to winds and pests, is not at all fussy about soil, even if it's heavy clay, and grows quickly. The white ash (*F. americana*) has a rounded shape, reaches a height of 15 to 21 m (50 to 70 feet) and a spread of 10 m (30 feet), and is hardy to Zone 3. Green ash (*F. pennsylvanica lanceolata*) has a spreading form, grows to 12 to 15 m (40 to 50 feet), and is hardy to Zone 2.

- Beech (*Fagus*): This native Canadian is shallow rooted and needs room to spread its roots. American beech (*F. grandifolia*) has a pyramidal shape, grows to 18 to 30 m (60 to 100 feet) with a spread of 15 m (33 feet), and is hardy to Zone 4.

- Canadian hemlock (*Tsuga canadensis*): This evergreen tolerates partial shade and likes cool, moist conditions. Use it as a specimen plant, or clip it for a hedge. It has a pyramidal shape, grows to 15 to 22.5 m (50 to 75 feet) with a spread of 7.5 to 10 m (25 to 35 feet), and is hardy to Zone 4.

- Catalpa (*Catalpa*): Large seed pods, 30 cm (1 foot) long, follow large white blooms in early summer. The heart-shaped leaves also add interest. The tree can be pruned into a neat shape with no harm. It withstands pests, drought and clay soil — another great performer. The northern catalpa (*C. speciosa*) has a rounded shape, grows to 12 to 21 m (40 to 70 feet) with a spread of 8 m (26 feet), and is hardy to Zone 5.

- Fir (*Abies*): Firs like cool, humid climates and need moist, well-drained acid soil. Although they will tolerate some shade, they do best in full sun. The Fraser fir (*A. fraseri*) has a slow growth rate. It's not at its best in cities, as it does not put up with pollution very well. It has a pyramidal shape, grows to 10 to 15 m (30 to 40 feet), has a spread of 6 to 7.5 m (20 to 25 feet), and is hardy to Zone 3.

🌿 Linden (*Tilia*): The little leaf linden (*T. cordata*) produces yellow fragrant flowers in early summer; the foliage is heart shaped and turns yellow in the fall. It's very tolerant of pollution, making it a good city tree. Pyramidal in shape, it grows to 9 to 18 m (30 to 60 feet) with a spread of 15 m (50 feet), and is hardy to Zone 3.

🌿 Locust (*Gleditsia*): This is a nice shade tree for the lawn — it has open branches that make filtered shade, allowing grass to grow underneath. To reach its maximum height, it should be planted in full sun. The sunburst locust (*G. triacanthos* 'Sunburst') has spreading branches, grows to 7.5 to 15 m (25 to 50 feet), and is hardy to Zone 5. Shademaster (*G. triancanthos* 'Shademaster') is rounded in shape, will reach 10.5 to 12 m (35 to 40 feet), and is hardy to Zone 4. Skyline (*G. triancanthos* 'Skyline') has a broad vase shape, grows to 9 to 10.5 m (30 to 35

feet), and is hardy to Zone 4. The spread for these trees is about 12 m (40 feet).

🌿 Mountain ash (*Sorbus*): In late spring, large white clusters of blossoms appear on the mountain ash, followed by red berries. The tree prefers acid, well-drained soil and full sun. The European mountain ash (*S. aucuporia*) has a rounded shape, grows to 4.5 to 10.5 m (15 to 35 feet) with a spread of 6 m (20 feet), and is hardy to Zone 3.

Shrubs and Hedges

Shrubs are amazingly useful — they can anchor a design, create a transition from one part of the garden to another, act as background, be a focal point, and more. They are often used as hedging material. Although hedges can be high maintenance, many people are willing to give them the attention they need to always look their best. Of course, you can grow a more informal hedge — more properly called a screen than a hedge — from many trees and shrubs. They'll still need some pruning attention but not the dedicated clipping that a formal hedge needs. A well-maintained and

---

Shrubs for Special Effects and Situations

Sun: beauty bush, buddleia, caragana, dogwood, forsythia, Japanese quince, rose of Sharon.

Shade: dogwood, forsythia, hydrangea, Japanese maple, double mock orange, mountain laurel, Oregon grape, highbush cranberry, Japanese kerria.

Dry soil: beauty bush, caragana.

Moist soil: dogwood, viburnum.

Acid soil: Japanese maple, mountain laurel.

Alkaline soil: rose of Sharon, buddleia, lilac, flowering crabapple.

Sandy soil: beauty bush, buddleia, mock orange.

Clay soil: forsythia, weigela, viburnum.

Winter interest: beauty bush, dogwood, Japanese maple, oakleaf and climbing hydrangea, mountain laurel, Oregon grape, virburnum.

Hedging material: Japanese quince, caragana, privet, boxwood.

pruned cedar hedge is one of the loveliest backdrops for a perennial bed and serves other functions as well, such as providing privacy and shelter. We all have garden jobs that don't really feel like chores to us, and trimming a hedge might be your favourite and most satisfying thing to do in the garden. But if you're a beginner gardener, it's safer to stay away from these high-maintenance features until you're really sure that's what you want.

Plant hedges in a single row or double staggered rows. The double staggered row produces a strong, dense hedge and will seem to fill in more quickly.

An intensive planting helps prevent erosion on slopes. It also cuts down weeding, which can be difficult on banks.

When pruning a hedge, make the bottom wider than the top. This will allow light and air to get into the interior.

The following plants make good hedges:

- European beech: a deciduous plant that holds on to some of its brown leaves into the winter.

- Boxwood: makes a beautiful slow-growing thick evergreen hedge that may need some winter protection in very cold areas.

- Cypress: evergreen, quick growing, needs more frequent clipping.

- Yew: makes a dense evergreen hedge and is relatively slow growing, thus requiring infrequent clipping.

  - Hawthorn: deciduous, its thorns act as an effective animal control.

  - Caragana: another deciduous plant that's a good choice for dry regions such as the prairies.

  - Privet: deciduous shrub that thickens well and produces small white flowers.

  The following shrubs are some of my favourites.

  - Beauty bush (*Kolkwitzi*a): The lovely upright growth and arching form of this shrub provide a nice accent in the garden, whether at the back of the border, as a stand-alone specimen, or as an informal hedge. In early summer, its bell-shaped flowers bloom in a soft pink with yellow throats, and in winter the peeling, silver-brown bark adds texture. Give it full sun, and although it will grow in most soils, it does best in dry sandy soil. Height: 3 m (10 feet); spread: 2.5 m (8 feet). Zone 5.

- Butterfly bush (*Buddleia*): Though it's slow to get started in the spring, the growth of the butterfly bush takes off in the summer, and by mid-summer it's covered in fragrant mauve, wine-coloured, or white spikes made up of tiny flowers. All have silver-grey foliage. As its name suggests, it attracts

I call the Buddleia a butterfly magnet, based on our experience every summer at our garden centres. When the bush comes into bloom, butterflies manage to find and feed on them in spite of the fact that we have more than 10,000 other plants in stock at the time!

butterflies. Some varieties have an attractive fountain shape; others can be a bit more unruly. Dwarf varieties are suited to the flowerbed and the small garden; the full-sized ones need a large garden. All varieties need to be cut back in mid-spring. It prefers full sun and well-drained slightly alkaline soil. Height: 3 to 4.5 m (10 to 15 feet); spread: 2.5 to 3 m (8 to 10 feet). Zone 5.

- Caragana (*Caragana*): This plant, also called pea shrub, is used extensively in the western part of Canada as hedging and screening material, shelter belts, and as snowtraps, which act like snow fencing to prevent drifting. It withstands drought, salty conditions, and poor soil extremely well — and not only that but it's attractive too. The foliage is rather ferny, and small, pea-shaped scented yellow flowers appear in the spring. Although it does best in full sun, it will tolerate some shade. Many varieties are available. Try the weeping variety, 'Pendula', for a specimen worthy of attention or marching in a row along a path. Height: 2 m (6 feet); spread: 2 m (6 feet). Zone 2.

- Dogwood (*Cornus*): Of the many dogwoods, the pagoda dogwood (*Cornus alterniflolia*) makes a great addition to the large garden where winter interest is desired. Its branches are decidedly horizontal, making a lovely silhouette against the snow. Fairly insignificant creamy flowers appear in the spring, followed by blue-black berries. Its light green leaves turn red in the fall, so it earns its keep in more than one season. Grow dogwoods in full sun or partial

shade; most of them prefer moisture-retentive soil; the red osier dogwood (*C. stolonifera*) particularly needs damp soil. Height: 4.5 to 6 m (15 to 20 feet); spread: 9 m (30 feet). Zone 2, depending on variety.

🌿 Forsythia (*Forsythia*): This shrub can be counted on for an outstanding show in early spring. Its arching branches are full of bright yellow flowers before its leaves come out. Once the flowering is done, the shrub seems to retreat to the background, so it's not a good choice for

Flowering fruit trees, whether viewed from afar or close up, help the gardener celebrate spring.

a focal point. Its fountain shape lends it to being underplanted with bulbs, followed on by shorter perennials or annuals. Plant in full sun or partial shade in average soil. It withstands air pollution well. Choose the variety carefully, as the hardiness varies greatly. I like *F. ovata* 'Ottawa'. Height: 1.8 to 3.5 m (6 to 12 feet); spread: 1.2 to 2.5 m (4 to 8 feet). Zone 4, depending on variety.

🌿 Hydrangea (*Hydrangea*): Here's another great shade lover that comes in all kinds of shapes and forms. Climbing hydrangea, considered a vine rather than a shrub, can go to 24 m (80 feet) but the popular shrub Peegee hydrangea is a reasonable 1.5 to 2.5 m (5 to 8 feet) in height and spread. It's also the hardiest hydrangea, hardy to Zone 3. Hydrangeas bloom in early summer to early fall, depending on the variety. Oakleaf hydrangea (*H. quercifolia*) has large, oak-shaped leaves that turn bright orange-red in the autumn. Its full white flower heads become pink over the season, going brown in the winter. It's quite an easy-care plant, as it is slow growing and doesn't need to be pruned. Give hydrangeas rich soil for best results, but they will tolerate a wide range. Zone 3, depending on variety.

Japanese maple (*Acer palmatum*): Use a Japanese maple as part of a larger landscape plan or as a focal point. Planted with other material, it will still be rather dominating, especially if the variety is one that colours brightly in the autumn or has the graceful sweeping branches common to these small trees. Some varieties grow to about 6 m (20 feet), and others only to 1 m (3 feet); the spread likewise varies greatly with variety. Grow it in dappled shade and shelter it from cold winds — protect it with two layers of burlap in Zone 5. The graceful branches show well against snow; their lacy foliage looks fabulous in the summer. Give it slightly acid soil. Zone 5.

Japanese or flowering quince (*Chaenomeles japonica*): At any other time than the spring, this quince is quite unobtrusive. But in the spring, its white, pinkish red, or orange flowers open just

before or after leaves unfold. In mild zones, the flowers can appear as early as January. This easy-to-grow shrub also makes a good pruned or unpruned hedge; the varieties with thorns are good if a barrier is desired — they are nasty! Plant it in full sun, in average dry or moist soil. Height: 90 cm (3 feet); spread: 60 to 90 cm (2 to 3 feet). Zone 5.

Japanese kerria (*Kerria japonica*): Partial, light, or full shade is best for this deciduous shrub. Its stiff upright growth looks good against a wall, and the stems provide winter interest by staying green year-round. Bright yellow flowers appear in the spring and last for a couple of weeks. Grow in moist fertile soil in partial shade. Height: 1.5 to 2 m (5 to 6 1/2 feet); spread: 1.8 m (6 feet). Zone 4.

Mock orange (*Philadelphus*): Many varieties are available, but the most common, the double mock orange, has an upright growth with curving, arching branches. Not only will it grow in partial shade, but its white flowers, which bloom in late spring and early summer, fill the air with a delicious fragrance. Prune mock orange back after flowering — it will bloom on the new wood. *Philadelphus virginalis*, with its drooping branches and double flowers, is worth seeking out. No special soil requirements. Zone 3, depending on variety.

Mountain laurel (*Kalmia*): This evergreen shrub makes a wonderful ornamental addition to the garden. Its showy flowers, which appear in early summer, are white shading to rosy. Its

branches become gnarled with age, making it of interest in the garden in winter, especially when grown with other evergreens or planted under tall oaks, which provide the conditions in which it will thrive: partial shade and acid soil. The soil should be moist but well drained. Height: 4.5 m (15 feet); spread: 2.5 m (8 feet). Zone 5.

🌺 Oregon grape (*Mahonia aquifolium*): This evergreen shrub can also make a good ground cover; in well-drained soil it will spread quickly by suckers. In other words, be sure you place it where you don't mind it growing rather vigorously. On the other hand, pruning it judiciously will keep it under control. Its advantages in the landscape are that it maintains its leaves in the winter, providing some interest at that season; it has bright yellow flowers followed by blue-black or red berries; massed, it

Vines are incredibly useful in the garden. Annual vines can provide a quick and temporary coverup until slower-growing perennial vines take over.

makes an attractive foundation planting. It can also be used in a woodland garden and makes a good screen and barrier hedge. Plant in partial shade in moisture-retentive soil. Height: 90 to 120 cm (3 to 4 feet); spread: 90 to 120 cm (3 to 4 feet). Zone 5.

🌺 Rose of Sharon (*Hibiscus syriacus*): Just when you're feeling down in the dumps about the garden towards the end of summer, the rose of Sharon starts blooming and makes you feel better. It's covered with masses of flowers — you can choose from a wide range, blue, white, purple, rose, pale pink — and the throats often have a contrasting colour. 'Blushing Bride' is soft pink with fully

double flowers, 'Minerva' has a deep red eye and soft lavender petals, and 'Helene' is white with a deep reddish-purple eye. The shrub has a neat, contained, upright growth that makes it a good choice as a specimen. You can also train it as an espalier or prune it to a more treelike shape. Its foliage is a bit late in appearing in the spring so plant some bulbs at its feet to brighten its corner. Plant it in full sun or partial shade in well-drained soil. Height: 3.5 m (12 feet); spread: to 2 to 2.5 m (6 to 8 feet). Zone 5.

🌼 Viburnum (*Viburnum*): You're bound to find something useful and attractive in this large group of plants, especially if you have a shady spot that needs filling. Some viburnums are deciduous, some evergreen in Zone 6, so they have a place in the winter garden. Use them for hedging, as single specimens, or in a group. As if all that weren't enough, they also produce flowers, followed by berries, and have numerous shapes. My favourites are Korean spice, fragrant viburnum, and highbush cranberry. They're easygoing about the soil, tolerating both alkaline and acidic soil, with moderate moisture. Zone 2 or milder, depending on variety.

Vines and Climbers

Vertical interest can be added to your garden design by using vines and climbers. They also help soften harsh outlines, screen views, deflect the eye from an unattractive view, and give great value by not taking up too much ground space. Some are showy, and others are happy to stay in the background and provide a neutral green canvas against which other showier plants can parade.

To make a wall or trellis a feature or focal point of the garden, grow several different vines up it — combinations of clematis that flower in complementary colours both at the same time and at different times in the season for continuous interest. Or use different vines together — an evergreen climber such as euonymus with a clematis twining through it for year-round interest. When you choose a vine, take note of how it climbs — some vines cling, some twine, some grab on by their tendrils. Be sure you have the right kind of support for the kind of vine you choose.

Vines and Climbers for Special Situations

Sun: bittersweet, clematis, Dutchman's pipe, everlasting pea, golden hop, kiwi, morning glory, porcelain berry, roses, trumpet vine, wisteria, euonymus.

Shade: bittersweet, Dutchman's pipe, kiwi, trumpet vine, euonymus.

Moist soil: cup and saucer vine, Dutchman's pipe.

Alkaline soil: clematis, morning glory.

Winter interest: bittersweet, climbing hydrangea.

Annuals and Perennials

The challenge for the gardener interested in design is creating a setting to show off perennial plants when they're flowering, but making them an integral part of the design even when not in bloom. Annuals bridge gaps, make transitions between colour groupings, and provide cheerful colour all season long.

Fritillaria

Creeping Phlox

Blanketflower

Begonias

Balloon Flower

Snapdragons and Dusty Miller

Black-eyed Susan

Dahlia

🌸 Bittersweet (*Celastrus scandens*): Bittersweet is a wonderful addition for autumn interest. The small green flowers, which appear in the summer, are followed by round fruits in the autumn, which split open to show their orange interiors that surround scarlet seeds. I have met many people who have become disappointed by their "non-fruiting" bittersweet. Buy a male and female to ensure fruiting will occur, and buy from a reliable supplier. Plant in either sun or partial shade in ordinary soil. Deciduous twining perennial. Zone 3.

🌸 Clematis (*Clematis*): You can find a clematis for nearly every need in the garden: the varieties are practically endless, offering a rainbow of colours, flower sizes, flowering periods, and pruning needs. However, they like their roots kept cool, so plant around their base with hostas or daylilies. You can also use an attractive rock or ornament set in front of the stem to provide shade and coolness to the roots. Although clematis need their roots in the shade, they like their tops in the sun. They do best in alkaline soil. Deciduous perennial that climbs using tendrils. Zone 3, depending on variety.

🌸 Climbing hydrangea (*Hydrangea petiolaris*): Although this is a slow grower, once it's established it's a stunning addition to the shady garden. It needs a wall or fence to cling to with its small aerial roots. The leaves are shiny and rounded; the flower heads, which are large, lacy, and white, appear in early summer. The leaves often turn yellow before dropping in the fall. In the winter, the peeling rust-coloured bark provides some texture. A bonus for city dwellers is that the climbing hydrangea is quite tolerant of pollution. Deciduous perennial. Zone 5.

🌸 Cup and saucer vine (*Cobaea scandens*): This vine, although fast growing, can be slow to produce flowers, so it usually doesn't bloom until late in the summer — but that may suit your purposes if you need some colour at that time of year. It attaches itself to supports by its tendrils. The flowers are white, greenish purple, or mauve-pink, and cup-shaped. It grows best in rich moist soil. Annual.

🌸 Dutchman's pipe (*Aristolochia macrophylla*): The heart-shaped bright green leaves provide a nice thick screen. Small green-yellow or purple-brown tubular flowers open in mid to late summer, but this fast-growing twining plant is grown mainly for its foliage, which gives a nicely old-fashioned look to a porch or arbour — it was popular a century ago. It will grow in both full sun and partial shade in moist but well-drained soil. Perennial. Zone 4.

🌸 Everlasting pea (*Lathyrus latifolius*): This plant makes a good job of covering the lower parts of other climbers, which are sometimes a bit bare. Bluish green leaves and purple, white, pink, or red flowers stay for most of the summer. It can take a while to start growing, but once it's at home, it doesn't like to be disturbed. Plant in full sun in well-drained soil, and provide support for it to climb on. Perennial. Zone 5.

- 🌺 Golden hop (*Humulus lupulus*): A fast-growing twining climber, hop makes a good covering for a fence or pergola and an effective privacy screen. Its yellow-green leaves have three to five distinct lobes, and it produces fruit that can be used in dried arrangements. (An annual variety is Japanese hops [*H. japonicum*]. It starts slowly, then takes off. It needs a strong support for its dark green foliage.) Give it moist, fertile soil in full sun. Perennial. Zone 3.

- 🌺 Kiwi (*Actinidia*): This fast-growing twining climber has attractive foliage, espe-

cially if you can get one of the varieties that are tricoloured in green, white, and pink. If you're determined to have fruit, you need a male and female plant and endless patience. A kiwi will almost always take more than five years to flower and bear fruit. When it does flower, the blooms will appear in mid-summer and be small and greenish white. If you want to keep it in check,

As an exercise, sketch out shapes on your flowerbeds — mounds, sprawlers, verticals — then choose the plants to match the shape. You'll be working like a designer and producing a pleasing composition. Imagine what this bed would look like as a series of shapes.

plant in poor soil. It can be planted in full sun or partial shade. Perennial. Zone 4.

Feathery-foliaged plants such as astilbes or cosmos planted at the end of the garden will make the garden look longer. The wispiness of the leaves makes the plants appear to be farther away.

🌼 Morning glory (*Ipomea*): For a summer of colourful blooms — blue, white, pink, lavender, red — plant morning glories in soil that's not too rich in full sun. In addition, since each seed produces only one vine, you should plant several to get a better covering, especially if your aim is to hide an unpleasant view or boring wall. Annual.

🌼 Porcelain berry (*Ampelopsis brevipedunculata*): This vine is good for covering walls and has three- or five-lobed leaves that are dark green on top and paler underneath. The underside also has a hairy texture. The insignificant green flowers that appear in late summer are followed by masses of small fruits that change from white to deep purple. It can become invasive in all but the colder zones. Plant in full sun in any soil except very damp soil. Perennial with twining tendrils. Zone 5.

🌼 Roses (*Rosa*): There's nothing like a climbing or rambling rose to add a romantic touch to a garden, especially when it's tumbling over a decorative arbour or pergola. They look attractive with clematis, but generally roses are used as stand-alone features in the garden. Train the branches horizontally to get more blooms. There's a wide variety of colours and flowering periods to choose from, including ones bred in Canada specially to withstand the extreme winter cold experienced in

many parts of the country — look for the Explorer series with names such as 'John Cabot' and 'William Baffin'. Most roses need sun. Zones vary.

🌼 Trumpet vine (*Campsis radicans*): It's hard to believe this exotic-looking climber can withstand some fairly cold winters. It's the type of vine that doesn't lend itself easily to pairing with another because it's a rampant grower, and when it's in bloom in the summer it outshines everything near it with its trumpet-shaped orange or scarlet flowers. Prune it in the spring to keep it under control. Keep it well watered. Plant in

The texture of the plants, particularly the feathery astilbe and the evergreen, give a lightness to this shady border. The plants are anchored by the solid rock, which has its own soft texture.

sun or partial shade in any soil. Perennial; clings with rootlets. Zone 4.

🌼 Wisteria (*Wisteria*): The ultimate in delicate foliage and flowers, wisteria has a reputation for being balky. It can take years before a plant will flower, but once it produces those mauve or white

scented flowers in early summer, you'll see the wait was worthwhile. In the meantime, the deeply fringed leaves make a lovely covering. Plant in moist but well-drained soil in the sun. Perennial. Zone 4.

Perennials and Annuals

We've dealt with the bones of garden design, so now let's look at the great array of material available for the smaller details that will fill in and enhance the permanent parts of your garden. These plants will be vital in carrying out the colour scheme you've chosen and invaluable to add texture and contrast. Annuals are usually selected because they bloom all summer long and thus make a splashy show. Perennials, on the other hand, have to earn their keep in two categories — their bloom and their foliage — because many perennials have a relatively short period when they're in flower, and you want them to look good and add something to the garden when not in bloom.

I've chosen the following perennials and annuals for structural qualities to help you carry out your design (refer to Chapter 3 for plants divided into colour groupings). As with trees and shrubs, research the mature height and spread and sketch it in on your plans. When you plant perennials, you may find there are great gaps between the plants, but these barren spaces will quickly fill in as the plants mature, usually in about two to three years. Meanwhile, use annuals or short-lived perennials to give your flowerbeds a lush look while the perennials are getting established.

As you choose your plants, imagine how the plants will look with one another —

If your flowerbed is against a wall or fence, plan to put the taller plants at the back, mid-size in the middle, and shorter plants at the front.

think about their colour, shape and texture. (Refer to Chapter 3 again for inspiration.) Think of plant groupings as compositions of plants rather than collections of individual specimens. If visualizing the finished look is difficult for you, go on some garden tours and see what you like and don't like. Thumb through books and magazines to get ideas.

In the following lists, you'll find mainly quite hardy perennials, which will be the permanent plantings, but I've listed some annuals that can provide design interest to the flowerbed, especially if your garden is young. The list is by no means encyclopaedic — more a tantalizing taste of the many, many plants from which you can choose.

🌿 Achillea (*Achillea*): Achillea, also known by its common name, yarrow, is a drought-tolerant perennial that adds mid-summer colour — white, yellow, pinkish rose, red, and soft pastels — to the middle or back of the border. Its aromatic feathery silver-grey foliage provides a lovely accent and softens bolder textures. Plant it in full sun in well-drained soil. Height: 20 to 120 cm (8 inches to 4 feet); spread: 30 to 90 cm (1 to 3 feet). Perennial. Zone 2.

🌿 Astilbe (*Astilbe*): Astilbes have interest at just about any time of year. In the spring, the hairy stems unfurl, glowing

Annuals and Perennials for Special Situations

Sun: acanthus, achillea, bugleweed, cosmos, creeping phlox, daylilies, nigella, ornamental rhubarb, pinks, yucca, coreopsis, black-eyed Susan, monarda, liatris, butterfly weed.

Shade: astilbe, bergenia, bleeding heart, epimedium, ferns, hosta, lamium.

Dry soil: achillea, cosmos, epimedium (once established), eryngium, nigella, pinks, yucca, impatiens, black-eyed Susan, monarda, coreopsis, liatris, lamium, sedum.

Moist soil: astilbe, epimedium, hosta, ligularia, ornamental rhubarb, impatiens, Joe-pye weed, swamp milkweed, iris, primula.

Sandy soil: achillea, cosmos, eryngium, pinks, yucca, nasturtium, poppy, sedum, portulaca.

Clay soil: daylily, monarda, aster, sneezeweed, Japanese anemone, Joe-pye weed, mayapple.

Alkaline soil: eryngium, foxtail lily, globe thistle, iris, poppies, scabiosa, morning glory, pasque flower, dianthus, maidenhair fern.

Acid soil: lupine, tiger lilies, butterfly weed, primula, trillium.

Feathery foliage: achillea, astilbe, cosmos, ferns, nigella, thread-leaf coreopsis, butterfly weed.

Large leaves: bergenia, hosta, ligularia, ornamental rhubarb, comfrey, foxglove.

Long narrow foliage: daylily, yucca, ornamental grasses, bamboo.

Back of the border: eryngium, foxglove, ligularia, lupine, yucca, Joe-pye weed, New England aster, delphinium, foxtail lily, sunflower.

Middle of the border: achillea, astilbe, bleeding heart, cosmos, daylilies, hosta, nigella, black-eyed Susan, monarda, liatris, coreopsis, butterfly weed.

Front of the border: bugleweed, bergenia, creeping phlox, epimedium, lamium, pinks, candytuft, miniature dianthus.

in the spring sunlight. In the summer, it's the soft feathery foliage and plumes of flowers in white, pink, red, or yellow that are the attraction. The foliage remains of interest into the fall, as do the dried flowerheads, which look delicate against a drift of snow. Plant in sun or dappled shade. They particularly like moist soil, and will do extremely well in boggy areas or along a stream. Height: 45 to 120 cm (18 inches to 4 feet); spread: 30 to 75 cm (12 to 30 inches). Perennial. Zone 4.

🌱 Bergenia (*Bergenia*): Bergenia's common name, heartleaf, gives you a clue about the shape of its leaves, though its crinkly, leathery leaves are somewhat rounder than a Valentine heart. This

A bright late-summer composition. Ensuring colour from early spring to late fall can be a challenge, but it's possible to plan for colour in the garden all season long, even using only perennials. These cheerful black-eyed Susans come into their own when many other perennials have finished.

plant does well as an underplanting, especially when combined with ferns and forget-me-nots in a shady spot — under a shrub, for example. In the very early spring, it throws up clusters of pink, rosy, or white flowers. Once the snow melts in spring, the evergreen foliage adds attractive colour. Plant in shade in nearly any kind of soil. Height:

45 to 60 cm (18 to 24 inches); spread: 60 cm (24 inches). Perennial. Zone 2.

🌸 Bleeding heart (*Dicentra spectabilis*): The arched stems of bleeding heart bear heart-shaped white or pink flowers in the spring. The leaves are delicate, elegant, and feathery and contrast nicely with ferns and hostas. Light shade will guarantee the plant will thrive, although many varieties are dormant by the middle of the summer. For six to eight weeks of flowers amid gorgeous fernlike foliage, look for *D. spectabilis* 'Luxuriant'. If your bleeding heart dies back after flowering, plant some shade-loving annuals near it, or a later-flowering perennial such as Japanese anemone. Height: 20 to 90 cm (8 to 36 inches); spread: 30 to 60 cm (12 to 24 inches). Perennial. Zone 3.

🌸 Bugleweed (*Ajuga reptans*): This easy-to-grow, quickly spreading perennial has glossy green, variegated, or bronze leaves and pink, blue, or white flowers. It's good in the rock garden or as ground cover and does best in full sun, although it will tolerate some shade and most soils. Height: 15 to 22 cm (6 to 9 inches); 15 to 22 cm spread: (6 to 9 inches). Perennial. Zone 2.

🌸 Cosmos (*Cosmos*): Cosmos look wonderful massed together or scattered throughout a cheerful cottagey garden. Swaying in the summer breeze, they add height and movement as well as colour, for they come in pink, white, burgundy, and shorter varieties are available in yellows and oranges. Their ferny foliage can stand on its own, so even before they begin to flower, they work to fill up empty spaces and provide lovely textures. They self-seed like crazy, so once you've got them it takes diligence to keep next year's seedlings under control. My favourite variety is 'Seashells' — its tube-shaped petals look gorgeous, and it's a prolific bloomer. Cosmos love the sun and dry soil. Height: 45 to 120 cm (1 1/2 to 4 feet); spread 45 to 60 cm (1 1/2 to 2 feet). Annual.

🌸 Creeping phlox (*Phlox subulata*): This plant gives a great hit of colour in the spring border or rock garden. Its needlelike green foliage is covered with masses of red, pink, white, or blue flowers. Put it in a sunny spot in well-drained soil. Height: 15 cm (6 inches); spread: 30 to 60 cm (1 to 2 feet). Perennial. Zone 2.

🌸 Daylilies (*Hemerocallis*): No garden should be without daylilies — plan for as many as you can, perhaps even a bed devoted to them. That may sound like an extravagant thing to say for a plant whose individual blooms last only a day. But daylilies provide so many blooms that you'll soon forget about each flower's short life — besides, with the introduction of new varieties, you can plan for continuous daylily colour from June to September. You can find a daylily for nearly any spot in the border — back, middle, or front — but don't confine them to just a flowerbed. Even when they're not in bloom, they look wonderful massed together — along a path, by a fence, on a slope, as a foundation planting — because of their foliage.

All plants need some care once they're planted. When you've spent the time designing your garden and implementing the plan with plants, you want to keep your landscape in top-notch condition.

The flowers come in almost every colour of the rainbow, except blue, purple, and green. The graceful, tapering straplike leaves make a nice contrast to plants with larger leaves. Put them in full sun or partial shade. They'll produce more blooms if planted in soil that's enriched with humus and well mulched. Height: 40 to 120 cm (16 inches to 4 feet); spread: 60 to 120 cm (2 to 4 feet). Perennial. Zone 1.

Epimedium (*Epimedium*): There's nothing particularly showy about epimedium (its common name is barrenwort — hardly inspiring), but it's a useful plant to introduce to the garden — at the base of walls, in front of shrubs, on rocky slopes, in shady gardens, especially with ferns and hostas. Its green leaves are an elongated heart shape, and some varieties have red margins and veins. In the spring it produces insignificant white, pink, violet, or yellow flowers. Plant it in sun or part shade in moist, humus-rich soil. It's a slow grower, but once it's established it can withstand drought. Height: 15 to 30 cm (6 to 12 inches); spread: 25 to 60 cm (10 to 24 inches). Perennial. Zone 5.

Eryngium (*Eryngium*): Depending on the variety, put eryngium, also known as sea holly, at the back or middle of the border. Some of the shorter varieties may tend to sprawl and thus benefit from the support of other plants or a bit of staking. Its decorative prickly foliage and purple-blue thistlelike heads perk up a late-summer garden. Plant it in the sun in any well-drained soil. Height: 60 to 90 cm (24 to 36 inches); spread: 30 cm (1 foot). Perennial. Zone 5.

Ferns: Ferns and shade are made for each other, and their feathery fronds help to lighten what might otherwise be a gloomy area. You can find a fern for nearly any situation from deep to light shade (even sun), moist to dry soil. In addition to their usefulness in the shade or natural garden, they can be planted in masses in difficult-to-deal-with spots such as a narrow passage between two houses or a slope. Planted with spring bulbs, they will grow up just as the bulbs' foliage needs hiding. For damp spots, try the Christmas fern, lady fern, and sensitive fern; for dry areas, rock fern, hay-scented fern, and marginal fern; for a sunny spot, hay-scented fern, bracken fern, Christmas fern. Heights and spread vary, as do zones.

- Foxglove (*Digitalis*): This is a natural for the English-country-garden look, with its tall flower spikes in a wonderful range of colours — white, pink, brown, raspberry, apricot. Mass them at the back of a shady border or let them grow up through rose bushes or other mid-size shrubs. They'll bloom in early to mid-summer. Plant in partial shade or sun in rich soil. Biennial; some will self-seed. Height: 90 to 150 cm (3 to 5 feet); spread: 30 to 45 cm (1 to 1/2 feet). Zone 4.

- Hosta (*Hosta*): Hostas have strongly architectural forms, and many have textured surfaces. They come in a great variety of blues, greens, and golds — there are more than 1,800 named varieties. Like daylilies, you can find a hosta in nearly any height you want, so don't use them only in the middle of the border. Their uses in the garden are many: massed, planted with ferns and wildflowers, under large trees, along a shady walk or driveway. They're especially good at growing over the dying foliage of spring bulbs. To make a bold statement, look for larger-leaved varieties such as *Hosta sieboldiana.* Plant them in the shade in rich soil that holds moisture well. Height: 10 to 60 cm (6 to 24 inches); spread: 30 to 120 cm (1 to 4 feet). Perennial. Zone 3.

- Lamium (*Lamium*): Lamium, also known commonly as spotted dead nettle, makes a very attractive ground cover, especially in English cottage gardens or informal gardens. It can become invasive, but judicious cutting back will control it. Its white-flecked leaves look particularly nice creeping over flagstones. Another advantage is that it will grow in dry shade. Height: 30 to 60 cm (1 to 2 feet); spread: 30 cm (1 foot). Perennial. Zone 2.

- Ligularia (*Ligularia*): This bold plant is best for the back of a border, especially where there's room for its large crinkly heart-shaped leaves and towering spikes of flowers. The orange-yellow flowers appear in mid-summer. It likes full sun or partial shade and moist soil and in fact is usually found near water gardens and in bog gardens. Height: 90 to 120 cm (3 to 4 feet); spread: 60 to 90 cm (2 to 3 feet). Perennial. Zone 5 or 6, depending on variety.

- Lupine (*Lupinus*): The spires of lupines, with their densely packed flower heads, look especially at home in a country or English cottage garden. They make a striking display when they bloom in early summer if they're planted in a mass. Blooms are white, cream, yellow, pink, purple red, or blue, with some bicolour combinations. Give them moist soil in light shade or sun. Height: 45 to 90 cm (1 1/2 to 3 feet); spread: 15 to 45 cm (6 inches to 1 1/2 feet). Perennial. Zone 2.

- Nigella (*Nigella*): Nigella also goes by the romantic name of love-in-a-mist. It has feathery bright green leaves, small pale blue flowers in the spring, frothy foliage. Nigella makes a good filler. After flowering, if you don't deadhead it, its seedpods will add decoration to the garden too. It likes sunny borders with soil on the dry side. Height: 40 to 45 cm (16 inches to 1 1/2 feet); spread: 22 to 30 cm (9 to 12 inches). Annual.

🌺 Ornamental rhubarb (*Rheum palmatum*): Don't try this plant in a small garden, but for a larger property, especially one with a stream or boggy area, it will make a bold statement. The highly decorative, deeply cut leaves and tall branching flower spikes, which bloom in early summer, are what make this plant of interest, and it makes an impressive focal point. Grow it in full sun or partial shade, and give it lots of moisture. Height: 1.8 to 3 m (6 to 10 feet); spread: 1.2 to 1.8 m (4 to 6 feet). Perennial. Zone 5.

🌺 Pinks (*Dianthus*): Pinks are at home at the front of a sunny well-drained border or in a rock garden. They are covered in blooms in late spring and are wonderfully fragrant. Choose from pink, purple, red, white, and bicolours. Their spiky blue-green foliage looks pleasing even when the plant isn't blooming. Height: 7.5 to 50 cm (3 inches to 2 feet); spread: 30 cm (1 foot). Short-lived perennial. Zone 4.

🌺 Yucca (*Yucca*): A statuesque evergreen plant, yucca makes a good foil for softer plantings. The foliage is spiky and sword shaped, and the amazing white flowers can shoot up to 1.8 m (6 feet). Because of its dramatic looks, it's sometimes hard to know what to pair with

Winter is the time when parts of the landscape that seemed unremarkable in summer take on a new importance. Plan for at least one feature that will look good in the winter.

the yucca. Try it in a bed of ornamental grasses, with succulents or low-growing junipers. It's tolerant of drought and loves the sun. Height: 90 to 180 cm (3 to 6 feet); spread: 90 to 120 cm (3 to 4 feet). Perennial. Zone 4.

Planting for the Changing Seasons

At some time or other, from spring to fall, most of us look at the garden and bemoan the lack of colour. How could we have planned so poorly, we wonder. Ensuring that the garden is full of colour during the gardening season is a challenge, but with the use of annuals we're usually able to overcome most of those lulls. But if you're relying only on perennials, including bulbs, it can be more difficult. Here are some plant lists for you to think about for your three seasons of colour. You may find that in your area some of the plants bloom a bit earlier or later than I've indicated, but the sequence of bloom is more important than when everything gets started.

Early spring
- Bulbs: snowdrops, crocuses, hyacinths, early tulips, anemone.

Spring
- Bulbs: daffodils, mid-spring tulips, scilla.

- Perennials and ground covers: rock cress, basket of gold, bleeding heart, bergenia, sweet woodruff, primroses, pasque flower, foamflower.

- Shrubs: lilac, rhododendron, highbush cranberry, forsythia, Tartarian dogwood.

Late spring/early summer
- Bulbs: allium, lily of the valley, late tulips.

- Perennials and ground covers: bellflower, snow-in-summer, bearded iris, flax, oriental poppies, phlox, vinca, peony, astilbe, lupine, daisy, pinks, coralbells, columbine, baby's breath.

- Shrubs: rhododendron, forsythia, Japanese kerria.

- Vines: climbing hydrangea, wisteria, clematis, silver lace vine.

Mid-summer
- Perennials: achillea, astilbe, daylily, veronica, liatris, balloon flower, coreopsis, thrift, Carpathian harebell, bellflower, pinks, cranesbill, monarda, evening primrose, Russian sage, lavender, baby's breath, butterfly weed.

- Shrubs: roses, lacecap hydrangea, peegee hydrangea, potentilla.

- Vines: clematis, trumpet vine.

Late summer/early fall
- Perennials: sedum, black-eyed Susan, daylily, chrysanthemum, globe thistle, evening primrose, Russian sage, boltonia, cardinal flower.

- Shrubs: roses, oak-leaf hydrangea, butterfly bush, burning bush (winged euonymus), Korean spice viburnum, rose of Sharon.

- Vines: roses, clematis.

Ready for a new season of gardening. Last year's landscaping is done and it's time to assess how it works. If you're like most of us, you'll be moving a few things — this isn't a sign of failure but a sign that you're an educated, observant gardener.

Fall

🌸 Perennials: aster, black-eyed Susan, goldenrod, coneflower, sneezeweed, Japanese anemone, boltonia.

🌸 Vines: autumn-flowering clematis, silver lace vine.

🌸 Shrubs (for berries): wintergreen, partridgeberry, firethorn, holly, cotoneaster.

In the preceding pages, I've touched on only a fraction of the plant material available for your garden. Each plant has its own requirements but from the selection I've given you, you can find a good array to fill in the final details of your garden design.

6

Garden Styles

By being familiar with some of the recognized garden styles of the past, you can be more knowledgeable about the design and planting of your own garden as you adapt the styles to your own conditions and situation.

A Bit of History

Not long ago, I visited the ancient city of Pompeii, which was covered by the volcanic ash of Mount Vesuvius in A.D. 79. Most interesting to me was a period garden that had been established in the courtyard of an estate that had belonged to a local wine merchant. This very formal garden was beautiful to look at and served a practical purpose as well. Most of the plants used in the design were herbs. They were fragrant, could be used in cooking, and made a living medicine cabinet — all at the same time. I am impressed by the resourcefulness of the earliest gardeners, a quality not lost on gardeners of today.

Gardening has a long tradition, going back before recorded history, when humans moved from a nomadic to a more settled agricultural life. The earliest gardens we know about were in Egypt about 3000 B.C. on the fertile soil along the Nile River. These first gardens were cultivated to provide food and were often dedicated to the gods, who, it was believed, gave life. From those beginnings in Egypt, gardening spread to Babylon, Persia, Greece, and Rome. As gardens and gardening evolved, agricultural techniques improved, hybridizing occurred, and new species were introduced.

Over the centuries, different regions and cultures became noted for particular styles of gardening. For example, from their beginnings, Egyptian gardens used water as an important element, for irrigation as well as for ponds. In Persia, gardens were enclosed by walls, to separate them from

We can pick and choose various elements from our favourite gardening period. In this modern setting, traditional features such as still water and natural rock are at ease with clean lines and spare plantings.

A bit of paradise right in the back yard. This resourceful gardener has taken advantage of the wall at the end of the garden to create the feeling of a sunken garden.

The word *paradise* comes from the Persian *pairidaeza,* which means "an enclosure."

the desert and to provide shade and coolness. They also used water channels, often arranged in terraces, around which the rest of the garden was designed. These irrigation channels lent the gardens a formal air, as they divided the gardens into geometrical shapes.

The Greeks adapted Persian ideas into their own gardens — after waging war on the Persians! — and the Romans in turn took the ideas even further, using the formal architectural flowerbeds, paths, pergolas, statuary, fountains, and pools in their

Korean boxwood, especially the hybrid varieties developed in Canada in recent years, is much hardier than its English cousins, some growing quite nicely in Zone 4. Protect all boxwood from harsh winter winds with a layer or two of burlap in late fall. In "snow-belt" country, it's best to build a plywood box around your boxwood for winter protection.

designs. The most popular flowers in the early centuries will be familiar to contemporary gardeners: violets, poppies, irises, lilies, and pansies. The Romans' influence was far-reaching because of the extent of their empire. Hadrian's Villa, a large country estate built at Tivoli, about 32 km (20 miles) outside Rome, by the emperor Hadrian between A.D. 118 and 138, had a great influence on future similar extravagant gardens for its use of monuments, buildings, and motifs that recalled glories of the past or other parts of the world.

Although most Canadian gardens don't recall glories of the past, our gardens do show direct links to the past. For example, patios were created by the Muslims at the beginning of the eighth century in southern Spain. When we plan formal gardens with carefully clipped hedges and symmetrical layouts, we are recreating, though on a much smaller scale, the great Renaissance gardens that began in Italy about the middle of the fifteenth century.

Today, as we plan and plant our gardens, we are in our small way carrying on the great tradition of gardening. Because the style of our gardens has changed over the years, garden fashions of the past are not always appropriate today. But by being familiar with some of the recognized garden styles of the past, you can be more knowledgeable about the design and planting of your own garden as you adapt the styles to your own conditions and situation.

The Italian and French Styles: The Formal Garden

When we talk of formal gardens, we are usually referring to the Italian and French styles of garden. These gardens are the ultimate in symmetry. They are noted for the way they divide space in geometrical shapes, almost overwhelming the role nature plays.

The classic Italian garden started in the Renaissance. It evolved from symmetrical plantings in geometrical shapes — circles, squares, triangles, and hexagons — to variations somewhat less rigid in layout but still with a central axis from which everything was laid out as if in mirror image. The architectural character of the gardens was closely related to the villas, casinos, and palaces around which they were constructed. The earliest Renaissance gardens were enclosed, but over time, holes were made in the walls to provide a view. In the fifteenth century, as newly wealthy merchants moved from Florence to the cooler hills of the vineyards outside the city, gardens were not enclosed, but were built on hillsides to take advantage of magnificent views.

These gardens used water lavishly — in cascades, fountains, dramatic waterfalls, and pools. On the other hand, plant material was used in a restrained fashion — hedges of boxwood or yew, very little grass, large gravel areas, and virtually no perennial flowers. Colour was supplied by climbing roses, pots of annuals, and sometimes parterre patterns of bedding plants (see page 148). Other elements, such as walls, stairways, and statuary, were fanciful and large.

The traditional French garden is an adaptation of the Italian. Like the Italians, in the fifteenth and sixteenth centuries the French began to move their gardens out from behind the walls of their chateaux and moats. The French continued the geometric patterns of beds and paths begun by the Italians, but they made the designs of the parterre beds more ornate and elaborate. Their sculptures and other ornamentation were more fanciful and romantic but smaller in scale. Water was not used as much as in Italian gardens, and grass replaced gravel. They also used trellis work, wall decorations, and garden pavilions.

Adapting the Formal Garden

Symmetry, simplicity, and repetition, either in plants or furnishings, are important aspects of the design of the classic formal garden. The "bones" of the garden are clear, and the structural qualities of the design are often more important than the plantings. The plantings are always seen in relation to the design as a whole, and they can serve to soften a design that seems too rigid in its execution.

The structure of the formal garden is made up of walls, evergreen hedges, paths and paving, and sculpture, which are enhanced by plants chosen for their shape, colour, and texture. In true French and Italian classic gardens, this "hard landscape" has been in existence for centuries and has an established and aged look to it, something that can be difficult to mimic in Canada, so approach this aspect of its design with some caution. However, most classical gardens are made over years, not over a weekend or even a season, so walls and paths will age naturally along with the rest of the garden. Paths surfaced with gravel or pebbles — typical materials in the classic formal garden — are not always practical for the Canadian climate, as they can make snow removal a problem. But many flagstones or precast fabricated materials are excellent alternatives.

As a bonus for the Canadian gardener, classical gardens, with their strong architectural elements, look good in the winter, even — or especially — covered with snow.

The English Landscape Movement

In the eighteenth century, Britons reacted against the formality and artificiality of Italian and French gardens. The romantic natural garden was espoused by painters, writers, and philosophers such as Jean-Jacques Rousseau. In an attempt to improve on nature, landscape designers introduced sweeping parklands to replace formal gardens. Everything was done on a grand scale: hills were built, valleys created, lakes dug, and straight paths and lines converted into curves. Paradoxically, the natural landscape was manipulated to make it look more natural!

Reproductions of classical buildings were erected, as well as temples, towers, instant "ruined" castles and grottoes. Because these constructions had no practical purpose, they were dubbed "follies" and were considered by some to have been built by people with more money than sense. Openness was a feature of the natural look, so fences were out. Instead, trees were planted to define the boundaries of a property, and ditches were dug to enclose animals. The look became so popular that it spread into Europe, in some cases resulting in the destruction of the older formal gardens, in other cases being incorporated to live happily beside the formal garden.

However, the formal garden is high maintenance. Even though there are no great expanses of lawn to cut or trees that will shed tons of leaves every autumn, many of the plantings will require much clipping and pruning to keep them looking top-notch.

Yew, an evergreen, is one of the basic plants used for hedging in the formal garden, as well as for topiary. It fills in very densely when pruned and can be clipped into straight lines, curves, or fanciful shapes. English boxwood is another evergreen that

We don't see much extravagant topiary in private gardens in Canada. But these amazing creations introduce an element of formality to the garden.

is a traditional hedging material for parterre designs. It is not as hardy as yew, but can be used to Zone 6. Rather than a hedge of boxwood or yew, make a slightly more informal and shorter hedge of euonymus trained and clipped to outline a bed.

Parterre Design

- Parterre is a stylized type of bedding or grouping of similar plants with the plants in each bed being of the same colour; the beds are geometric and ornamental and are separated from one another by paths or grassed areas.

- One common and pleasing parterre design is a grouping of four beds arranged symmetrically around a central ornamental feature such as a sundial or sculpture.

- The parterre beds are outlined by low formal trimmed hedges. Some appropriate materials for planting the hedges are dwarf boxwood (the traditional plant for parterre hedges), yew, santolina, or lavender. Inside, the pattern may be filled by grass or flowers. Annuals make better fillers because of their continuous bloom, providing colour throughout the season.

- Other possibilities for filling the interior of the hedged area: gravel; water; vegetables; herbs; low-growing shrubs or perennials.

- This type of design does not offer the opportunity to grow a wide variety of plants but is undertaken for the precision of its lines, the contrasts of colours that can be used, and the way it relates to its accompanying buildings.

- Today, parterre can be used with many modern buildings because its geometric basis complements these structures well.

The plants used to fill the parterre beds can be nearly anything that takes your fancy. Keep in mind that if you are strictly following the formal style, the idea is to fill the enclosed squares, rectangles, circles, and so forth with a single colour. So a mass of white pansies or salmon pink begonias is preferable to a mixture of multi-coloured flowers or different flowers entirely, if you are striving for an authentic feeling. As well, the flowers should not tower over the hedges, so tall plants such as delphiniums or cosmos are not appropriate. With careful planning, you can change the bed colour and planting scheme throughout the year. In spring, use any mass of similar-coloured bulbs — tulips, scillas, daffodils. In late spring, replace the bulbs with colourful annuals such as pansies and begonias, or try something different such as blue fescue, a short blue-grey ornamental grass. In the fall, some low-growing mums or ornamental cabbage will add new life to the parterre bed.

Incorporate water, whether it's in a still square or rectangular pond or running through a fountain. The fountain could be a focal point, for classical garden design lends itself readily to the use of a focal point. Other ideas for focal points could be an urn, a sundial, a statue, or a well-placed garden bench. A container that displays a clipped single specimen of boxwood or bay also makes a good focal point.

The English Style: The Cottage Garden

Gardening styles in England have gone through many transitions. We can trace the history from the enclosed medieval garden to the eighteenth-century landscape movement — a reaction against the artificiality of formal gardens — to the Victorian garden and then to the introduction of the type of

Parterre takes some upkeep but if you choose a slow-growing evergreen for the hedge, it will cut down on maintenance time.

garden most of us associate with the English, the cottage or country garden.

A cottage garden traditionally was the garden of the humbler folk. Such gardens were generally small and bright, nestled against cottages that were themselves small. The plantings were usually chosen because they were useful (for food, medicine, dyes) or because they were admired by the gardener. Plantings were often random, in a colourful and charming jumble. Paths were made of local materials, were relatively narrow, and had a practical purpose. Gates were simple and usually made of wood

Cheerful bright marigolds are at home in the cottage garden. Don't put them in rows — let them meander among other plants.

rather than metal. Fences similarly were rustic in nature and often were hedges to keep farm animals out and to mark the change from garden to countryside.

Adapting the Cottage Garden

In Canada, it's difficult to recreate the soft misty air that seems a part of the English landscape, but we can certainly use some of the traditional plants. This country also lacks the perfect accompaniment to the cottage garden — a thatched cottage! But many older Canadian houses, from urban bungalows to country farmhouses, are a perfect match for the cottage garden style.

To recreate the feel of an English cottage garden, throw formality out the window. The effect you're seeking is of a rich profusion of flowers — and they don't have to be only the old-fashioned favourites. Run them together in bold enthusiastic bunches; let them tumble into the paths and over edges of retaining walls or containers.

Lawns don't play a large role in a cottage garden. Trees should be fruit or nut trees or at least blossoming trees — apple, plum, pear, cherry, hazel, almond. Holly or yew are appropriate evergreens.

Most of the plants typical of the English cottage garden are at home on this side of the Atlantic. They are likely to have a longer period of dormancy than in the moderate climate of Great Britain, but once they get going, they'll rival anything you can find there. Herbaceous perennials are the mainstay of the cottage garden — foxgloves, hollyhocks, poppies, peonies, daisies, lupines, stocks, delphiniums, and irises are some plants that provide colour, movement, scent, and beautiful flowers. Incorporate vegetables and fruit bushes into the garden for a feeling of total harmony.

Colourful plants, including herbs such as chives, parsley, bergamot, lemon balm, and thyme, in simple containers by the front door are appropriate in this relaxed and unpretentious design. Scented plants such as lavender are also right at home in the cottage garden, as are climbing roses and honeysuckles.

Arbours, trellises, and furniture should all be of a simple or even rustic nature. Wood and stone are more appropriate materials than concrete or metal.

The Japanese Style

A Japanese garden is a place of tranquillity. Traditionally, every element symbolized some aspect of nature or human life. Today, the symbolism is less important, but the elements are still used because of their traditional and aesthetic connections. The guiding principles are order, harmony, and decorum, and the basic materials are water, plants, and stones.

The Japanese garden is private, restrained, full of contrasts of light and shade and hard and soft textures. Each element is placed so that it looks as if it's been there forever. The idea is to suggest nature rather than copy it.

Water is one of the most important elements in a Japanese garden. Used in waterfalls and water courses, it's meant to suggest high mountain streams. Bridges and stone lanterns represent a safe pathway. When water is not gently flowing in the Japanese garden, it is still — fountains are not used. However, water is not always present, and in these cases it is suggested by flowing white sand, gravel, or small stones. The impression of waves is created by raking the materials. Boulders often emerge from these constructed rivers, and stepping stones, both in real and implied streams, are often used.

The other important elements in the Japanese garden are stone and greenery. Flowers do not play a significant part, but when they are used, they are likely to be irises, peonies, lilies, or chrysanthemums,

Renovation of a Front Yard Garden

The front yard is the face we present to the public. From a design point of view, it's often been a neglected part of the property, but as we expand our gardening horizons, we naturally turn to the front yard. Many renovated front yards are exciting experiments in solving the problem of separating the house from the street, providing a transition from the public to the private, yet still remaining welcoming.

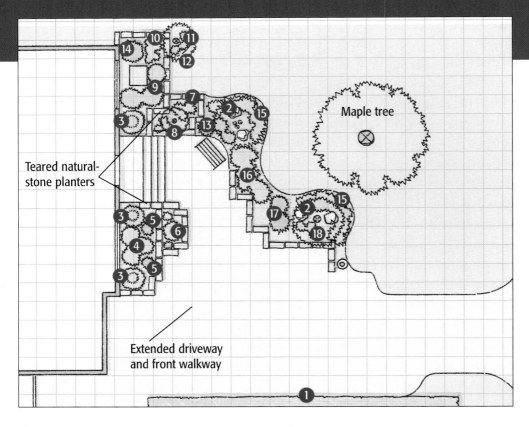

Teared natural-stone planters

Maple tree

Extended driveway and front walkway

1. Cedar (*Thuja occidentalis*)

2. Purpleleaf sand cherry (*Prunus cistena*)

3. Pyramid cedar (*Thuja occidentalis*)

4. Compact oregon grape (*Mahonia aquifolium*)

5. Sedum (*Sedum spectabile*)

6. Blue globe spruce (*Picea pungens*)

7. Juniper (*Juniperus horizontalis*)

8. Blue globe spruce standard (*Picea pungens*)

9. Hicks yew (*Taxus media* 'Hicks')

10. Astilbe (*Astilbe*)

11. Pee gee hydrangea standard (*Hydrangea paniculata* 'Grandiflora')

12. Hosta (*Hosta*)

13. Dakota charm spirea (*Spiraea bumalda* 'Dakota Charm')

14. Emerald gaiety Euonymus (*Euonymus fortunei* 'Emerald Gaiety')

15. Rockspray cotoneaster (*Cotoneaster*)

16. Mugho pine (*Pinus mugo mugo*)

17. Adam's needle (*Yucca filamentosa*)

18. Bergenia (*Bergenia*)

Echoes of the straight lines of the house are seen in the zigzag of the retaining wall. The soft colour of the paving stones and rocks is a good foil to the darker brick. The generous path directs your feet and eyes to the front entrance.

all of which are hardy in most parts of Canada. Stones or boulders are arranged in groups to represent mountains; flat stones can form a path.

Stone lanterns are placed by paths or bridges to give light to the visitor. Bridge railings and screens are frequently constructed of bamboo. Furniture is made of natural materials, and seats are usually low to the ground.

Straight lines are rarely found in a Japanese garden. Walls are not used very often, and separating one part of the garden from the other or separating the garden from the street or a neighbour's property is achieved by using fences of bamboo or screens of grasses.

Common plants in a Japanese garden are plum, cherry, maple, and bamboo. Pines and juniper may be clipped into floating cloud shapes. Rhododendrons and azaleas fit into the Japanese-style garden very nicely, as well. If your climate is accommodating (damp and shady), moss can be used as a "floor"; in sunnier situations, try woolly thyme. But keep in mind that all plant material is used sparingly.

Adapting the Japanese Style

If you love the idea of a Japanese garden but the demands of your lifestyle mean you need a kids' play area or a spot given over to the barbecue, don't despair. Japanese gardens are noted for their minimalist qualities, so claim a small section of the yard and make it your quiet place of contemplation. Some screening made of bamboo or rushes will separate it from the hurly-burly of the rest of the yard. Install a reflecting pool, bring in a piece of interesting driftwood, place some rocks strategically, and plant a couple of low-growing evergreens to bring

the elements of the Japanese garden to your backyard. A low wooden bench or even a low platform of slats of lovely wood will give you a place to sit. Add a single cushion or a bonsai plant on the corner of the bench or platform for the final touch. Above all, keep it simple — understatement is the key. There really isn't room for a bridge or teahouse in a small garden, but if you have the space, go for it!

Choose plants for their foliage. In our climate, you can rely on some old favourites — hostas, ferns, mugo pines, Japanese maples. Blossoming fruit trees such as cherry and plum can also be used.

The Modern Garden

The modern garden takes its inspiration from modern architecture. Because it's been designed to fit with today's architecture and is not as geographically specific in its plant use as other styles I've described, it needs no adaptation at all. You may, however, want to modify it for you own purposes. It's a garden style appropriate for houses with little ornamentation, and the bold, simple lines of the house are carried through to the garden. The modern style uses clean, hard landscaping materials and fewer plants than in most other styles of gardens. Lines and shapes are simple and geometric. It's one style that can easily incorporate modern features such as swimming pools, hot tubs, and Jacuzzis.

The plants also exhibit architectural qualities and are chosen more for their form and texture than their flowers. They have clean lines and bold foliage that contrasts with other plants or with the other garden features. Hostas and spiky plants such as grasses, yuccas, and even daylilies in bright clear colours will look good in a modern garden.

Cacti, with their unusual forms and textures, make attractive additions. In our Canadian climate, grow them in containers and bring them indoors in the winter.

The ground is usually covered with gravel, square or rectangular stones, or large slabs of cement rather than plant material. These hard substances can be used in conjunction with parterre plantings. Hard furnishing materials such as marble, slate, interlocking brick, and concrete can be used for paths, patios, and tabletops. Wood, as long as it has clean, hard edges and has its bark and knotty protrusions taken off, has a use in many situations in the modern garden — for decks, furniture, containers.

An informal planting will soften the edges of a formal house.

Ideas from the classical gardens and elements from Japanese gardens can be introduced into the modern garden without being jarring, but the busy nature of an English cottage garden would be out of place.

The modern style is suited to small areas, such as courtyards, where abstract or modern sculpture can make an effective focal point. In any modern garden, decoration and accessories are kept to a minimum and colours are crisp, clean, and often stongly contrasting.

7

Theme Gardens

We're always adapting our dreams to the reality of the situation. Here are some ideas for special gardens or gardening in special conditions.

Sometimes circumstances — shade, seaside climate, sandy soil — force us into a particular way of designing our garden. Or a particular interest pulls us in one direction — we want to grow vegetables that are pesticide-free, having a water garden has been a longtime dream, or we have fallen in love with alpine plants. We're always adapting our dreams to the reality of the situation. Here are some ideas for special gardens or gardening in special conditions.

Meadow Garden

A well-done meadow garden needs space; after all, that's what a meadow is — a wide-open space. I think of a meadow garden as a quilt of colours, the sections being large swathes of colourful plants all set on a background of grasses. Some people are attracted to a meadow garden because they're looking for a low-maintenance (sometimes even a no-maintenance) garden, and it's true that meadow gardens are easy-care landscapes. But if this type of garden is anywhere but in the country, some care will be needed to keep it within bounds; many of the plants used in the meadow garden are self-seeding and may be considered weeds by some. I like a meadow garden if you have lots of space and you want constant colour changes throughout the season — from the rich bright colours of the summer to the greys and yellows of late autumn.

Slopes can be challenges for gardeners. Erosion is a problem and accessibility may be difficult. But as this garden shows, there's scarcely a problem that can't be overcome while still maintaining variety in plant material and turning a potential problem into a beauty spot.

The meadow garden does best in full sun, and the plants are usually not fussy about the soil. The plants you'll choose are used to surviving without additional fertilizer or extra watering in times of drought — this is what gives the meadow garden its low-maintenance appeal. The meadow garden should be mowed once a year, in the late summer, after most plants have set seeds.

Meadow gardens often look best from a distance rather than close up and thus are often more appropriate on country properties. They can make a good transition between the garden and wilder parts of the landscape.

If you purchase a wildflower mix, be sure there are both annual and perennial seeds in it. The annuals can fill in while the perenni-

Even if you don't have a wildflower or meadow garden, introducing plants such as purple coneflower can give the flowerbed a "country" feel.

als get established, which can take a couple of years. If you're making your own "mix," look for wildflowers that are native to your region and use them in your meadow garden. Goldenrod, a native, and Queen Anne's lace, which is now found throughout North America but was imported from Europe, are two plants sometimes looked on as weeds, but they make an attractive addition.

Rather than using flowers, however, you could make a beautiful meadow garden with nothing but native grasses. Swathes of grasses moving in a gentle breeze are every

To some people, urban meadows can look like weed patches. Be sure to let your neighbours know what you're planning to do if you live in an urban area and want a bit of meadow in your front or backyard.

bit as lovely as masses of colourful flowers. If a whole meadow of grasses doesn't appeal to you, try a corner of grasses or use them as a transition from a more controlled part of the garden to the wilder section. Grasses are bound to make their way into your meadow over time. Don't discourage them, for they will set off the flowers nicely.

You can naturalize daffodils and other bulbs in a meadow garden and leave the grass to grow up around them, hiding their foliage. To make a stunning spring display, plant large areas. The best way to get such large quantities of bulbs planted is to invite your friends to a bulb-planting party — the job will be done in a day and your back will be in reasonable shape. For a large area, it's best to make a plan that takes into account the sequence of bloom and the colours if you're planting several types of bulbs. Choose bulbs with bright colours and big flowers since you'll most likely be viewing them from a distance. Plant them in large groupings for the best effect.

As I mentioned above, you can buy special wildflower mixes, make up your own, or buy seedlings. Here are some plants to look for.

- Asters (*Aster*): perennial

- Beebalm (*Monarda*): perennial

- Black-eyed Susan (*Rudbeckia hirta*): perennial and biennial varieties

- Blazing star (*Liatris*): perennial

- Butterfly weed (*Asclepia*s): perennial

- Cardinal flower (*Lobelia cardinalis*): perennial

- Clover (*Trifolium*): perennial

- Coreopsis (*Coreopsis*): annual and perennial varieties

- Goldenrod (*Solidago*): perennial

- Grasses such as northern sea oat (*Chasmanthium latifolium*) and canary grass (*Phalaris*)

- Lupine (*Lupinus*): perennial

- Poppies (*Papaver*): annual and perennial varieties

- Purple coneflower (*Echinacea*): perennial

- Queen Anne's lace (*Daucus carota*): biennial

The Shade Garden

I'm glad to see that shade has come into favour as gardeners discover the variety of plants that prefer protection from the brightness of the sun. Rather than being a design problem, shade introduces us to the subtleties of complementary greens and the contrast of texture and shape of leaves, opening up many design possibilities. The play of light and shadow beome a living part of the garden and its design, adding drama to the scene. In fact, in order to add interest to their gardens, some people bring shade into the garden by building arbours and covered areas or by planting fast-growing trees and shrubs.

If you've got dappled shade and moist conditions, you've got the foundation for a beautiful woodland garden. Large-leaved plants are particularly attractive in a

In damp climates, paths and patios in the shade can become quite slippery. If the paths, decks, or patios are to be used frequently, especially by children or elderly people, safety becomes a factor in the material used and the upkeep required to keep it in good condition. Under these circumstances, use a rough-surfaced material.

woodland garden when the light plays on them. A grouping of hostas and ferns provides nice contrasts in textures and leaf shapes. In the shade, pale-coloured flowers will show up better than dark reds and purples. The still, sheltered air of the woodland garden also holds the scent of fragrant flowers longer than in more open areas.

The most challenging shade of all is dense shade, especially dry dense shade such as that found under mature shade trees; even in such a difficult condition, there are plants you can use such as euphorbia and lamium. On the other hand, you may decide the best way to deal with this type of shade is not to plant it at all. If you are concerned that plants grown in deep and permanent shade, such as that cast by a building, will always look stunted and leggy, cover the ground with an attractive mulch such as shredded bark, small pebbles, or gravel. Or use a combination of mulch and brick or paving to make the area tidy and attractive. Another option is to have a set of containers that you rotate in the area — move some containers there for a few days, then bring them back into a

brighter section of the yard while another set of containers takes their place in the shade. If you do want to persevere with dry shade, though, you'll need to start enriching the soil. Dig in lots of compost and leaf mould every year to raise the nutrient content and the moisture-retention abilities. When I say lots, I mean at least 2.5 cm (1 inch) of finished compost spread over the area and turned under at least 15 cm (6 inches) — do this every year.

Rather than driving yourself crazy trying to grow grass in shady areas, use mulch under spreading trees, especially evergreens. Better yet, underplant them with some of the ground covers that thrive in shade: lily of the valley, pachysandra, lamium and euonymus are four of the many you can choose from.

Here is a list of some plants that do well in various shade conditions — I've included some trees and shrubs, as well. Growth will be less vigorous for some of these plants than if they were grown in more light; nevertheless, they will all perform admirably.

🌺 Astilbe (*Astilbe*): perennial; dappled damp shade

Types of Shade

Dappled shade: Created by the canopy of tree branches, dappled shade can be cool and dense in summer, almost nonexistent in late fall, winter, and early spring; makes for good woodland gardens.

Partial shade: Created when an area is in full sun for part of the day and in shade for the rest; length of time the area gets sun can have an important effect on whether plants will bloom.

Full shade: An area that is always in shadow but still receives enough diffused light to grow plants — for example, the north side of a wall in an otherwise open area.

Dense shade: Very little or no light penetrates to the ground; often also quite dry, as little rainfall can reach the ground either because of heavy growth or overhanging buildings.

- Bleeding heart (*Dicentra*): perennial; dappled shade

- Coleus (*Coleus*): annual; partial to full shade

- Epimedium (*Epimedium*): perennial; dry or damp shade

- Ferns: perennial; generally prefer damp shade but depends on variety

- Foamflower (*Tiarella*): perennial; partial or full shade

- Foxglove (*Digitalis*): biennial; partial or dappled shade

- Heartleaf bergenia (*Bergenia cordifolia*): perennial; partial shade

- Hosta (*Hosta*): perennial, moist dappled to full shade

- Impatiens (*Impatiens*): annual; dappled to full shade

- Japanese kerria (*Kerria japonica*): perennial; partial or full shade

- Lady's mantle (*Alchemilla*): perennial; dappled or partial damp shade

- Lamium (*Lamium*): perennial; dry shade

This gardener has natural shade and has taken advantage of it. If you want to introduce shade into your garden and don't want to wait for a tree to grow, a pergola with a fast-growing vine over it will provide shade.

Construction of a Shade Garden

1. Dense yew *(Taxus)*
2. Coral bells *(Heuchera sanguinea)*
3. Emerald gaiety euonymus *(Euonymus 'Emerald gaiety')*
4. Ferns
5. Japanese kerria *(Kerria japonica)*
6. Forget-me-not *(Myosotis)*
7. Hosta *(Hosta)*
8. Bergenia *(Bergenia)*
9. False spirea *(Sorbaria sorbifolia)*
10. Silverleaf dogwood *(Cornus 'Elegantissima')*
11. Red currant *(Ribes sanguineum)*
12. Slender deutzia *(Deutzia gracilis)*
13. Pee Gee hydrangea *(Hydrangea paniculata grandiflora)*
14. Bleeding heart *(Dicentra spectabilis)*
15. Virginia creeper *(Parthenocissus quinquefolia)*
16. Astilbe *(Astilbe)*
17. Trillium *(Trillium)*
18. Creeping cotoneaster *(Cotoneaster)*
19. Columbine *(Aquilegia canadensis)*
20. Purple fountain beech *(Fagus sylvatica 'Fountain')*
* Periwinkle *(Vinca minor)*

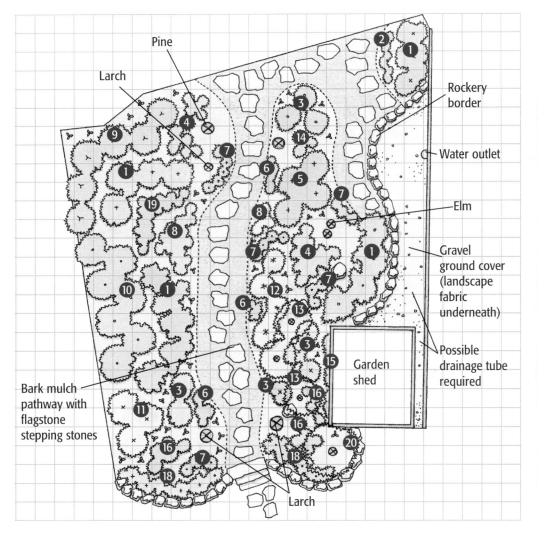

Firm and sturdy slabs of rock, well-anchored in the slope, promise a safe climb from one level to another. Good use has been made of existing plants — the trees contain the new path and guide the visitor's steps. As the new plantings take hold in the dappled light, the garden shed will become part of the background. The lower level provides a pretty view of the restful shades and textures of green.

Shade gardeners can choose from a wide range of ferns. Most ferns don't like to be kept too dry, so if you've got the right conditions, start a fern collection.

- Lobelia (*Lobelia*): annual; dappled to partial shade

- Oakleaf hydrangea (*Hydrangea quercifolia*): shrub; partial shade

- Periwinkle (*Vinca*): perennial; dense dry shade

- Virginia creeper (*Parthenocissus quinquefolia*): perennial vine; partial to full shade

The Environmentally Friendly Garden

The environmentally friendly garden is less a style than an attitude. We want our gardens to be in harmony not only with nature in the plants we choose but also in the way we maintain them. That means cutting down on chemicals in the garden. It's not always practical to avoid them completely, but one way of being a responsible gardener is to use plants that are not prone to disease and insect attack. Another way to be environmentally friendly is to keep watering to a minimum and to recycle rainwater. Installing a rain barrel is one way of capturing rainwater that would otherwise go into the sewer; if you want your garden to be as environmentally friendly as possible, add a spot for a rain barrel in your design. A clever idea is to have "water catchers" as part of your design, as well — above-ground basins or wells that can be topped up from full water barrels and used for dipping watering cans into. The still reflection of the water adds a peaceful note to the garden. Put a goldfish in each barrel or well to consume mosquito larvae.

Composting is an important activity in the environmentally friendly garden, so in your garden plans, make sure you have a good spot for at least one compost bin, though serious compost aficionados with the space will have two or three on the go at once. The garden design should use paths to make it easy to move from the composting and water-storage areas to the planted sections of the garden. In addition, the composting area should be easily accessible from the house, especially if you are composting throughout the winter. It's nice to have a spot where you can sieve your finished compost and perhaps even store it for next season. The material left over after sieving will make a good mulch. Annual additions of compost will keep the soil's fertility high. Mulching helps to retain moisture during dry periods and retards weed growth.

Shallow basins of water can catch rainfall but they also attract birds and wildlife to your garden. These creatures will help the ecosystem of your garden by feeding on insects. Even raccoons are helping when they dig in your lawn for grubs – you may not like the way the lawn looks, but those rascals are actually doing you a big favour by consuming the pests.

Lawns are great consumers of energy — yours and the kind that comes in a gasoline can. A push mower is a good alternative for the electric or gas-powered kind, unless you have large areas to mow (in which case, you might want to check back a few pages to the meadow garden for alternatives to large lawns). Ground covers can be used extensively to replace lawns, as well. However, a lawn has many uses, and especially if you have children, there's no better play surface. So if you want a lawn, learn to live with a few dandelions and bits of clover and hold off on the pesticides and herbicides. Set the mower blades high (5 to 6 cm/2 to 2 1/2 inches) so you don't scalp the lawn when you mow to help keep weeds in check. Water as infrequently as possible — no more than once a week — to encourage the grass to send roots deep into the soil, where they'll be less subjected to the stress of drought.

In the environmentally friendly garden, annual additions of compost at least 2.5 cm (1 inch) thick will keep the soil's fertility high. Mulching helps to retain moisture during dry periods and retards weed growth. Use fallen leaves to mulch perennial beds. Rake leaves into a long pile about 25 cm (5 inches) deep; set your power mower at its highest setting and run it over them. Rake these shredded leaves onto your perennial bed to a depth of 5 cm (2 inches). Earthworms will feed on them all summer long and you'll eliminate your weeding problems at the same time.

The environmentally friendly garden uses plants to save energy. Plant trees to protect the house from the summer sun. This can take a few years to pay off if the trees are immature, but in the long run, it's worth it. Trees can lower ambient temperatures by several degrees on a hot summer day. In addition, they help to muffle sound from the street, offer protection from the prevailing wind, and help clean the air. Sun porches on the south or west of the house will make the house cooler by cutting down on the amount of direct sun shining into the house.

Here are some plants that have low moisture requirements, but they all will look great in any garden. Silver- and grey-leaved plants are often drought tolerant — a bonus, since so many of them are attractive and enliven many colour schemes.

- Achillea (*Achillea*): perennial
- Artemisia (*Artemisia*): perennial
- Aster (*Aster*): perennial
- Catmint (*Nepeta faasenii*): perennial
- Coreopsis (*Coreopsis*): annual and perennial varieties
- Cotoneaster (*Cotoneaster*): shrub
- Euphorbia (*Euphorbia*): perennial
- Evening primrose (*Oenothera*): perennial
- Flax (*Linum*): perennial
- Flowering quince (*Chaenomeles*): perennial
- Globe thistle (*Echinops*): perennial
- Grape hyacinth (*Muscari*): perennial
- Lavender (*Lavandula*): perennial
- Lilac (*Syringa*): shrub
- Morning glory (*Ipomoea*): annual vine

Unless you are willing to invest a lot of time (and some money!) in a "shade-tolerant" lawn, I discourage you from trying. There are no grasses that love the shade and very few that tolerate more than half a day of it. If you choose to try growing grass in the shade, I suggest you look for a blend of grass seeds that includes at least 50 per cent red fescue. And plan on overseeding the area every spring or early fall.

- Pasqueflower (*Pulsatilla*): perennial

- Penstemon (*Penstemon*): perennial

- Potentilla (*Potentilla*): shrub

- Prickly poppy (*Argemone*): perennial

- Purple coneflower (*Echinacea*): perennial

- Russian olive (*Elaeagnus*): deciduous tree

- Scotch pine (*Pinus sylvestris*): evergreen tree

- Sedum (*Sedum*): perennial

- Serviceberry (*Amelanchier*): shrub

- Silver lace vine (*Polygonum*): perennial vine

- Sumac (*Rhus*): deciduous shrub

- Statice (*Limonium*): annual, biennial, and perennial varieties

- Sweet William (*Dianthus barbatus*): biennial

- Thrift (*Armeria*): perennial

- Trumpet vine (*Campsis*): perennial vine

- Virginia creeper (*Parthenocissus quinquefolia*): perennial vine

- Yew (*Taxus*): shrubs and trees

Attracting wildlife to the garden is an important aim of many gardeners. Plant shrubs and trees that provide protection and fruits and berries for creatures to eat.

The Low-Maintenance Garden

Let's face it — we all lead busy lives and as much as we love gardening, there are other things that need our attention too. So I have great sympathy for people who sometimes feel guilty about time spent in the garden. It's easy to build into your design some low-maintenance features, though — and it's better to do it now, at the planning stage, than later.

The best way to save time in the garden, and still have it look lovely, is to keep maintenance chores to a minimum. That doesn't mean letting nature run rampant, but it means designing your garden for easy care and choosing plants that don't need a lot of deadheading, watering, staking, and so forth to stay in the best of health.

Patios, decks, and even ground covers are easier to look after than a lawn is. But if you do want a lawn, or don't want to get rid of your current one, pay attention to the mowing strip — that is, that place where the lawn meets the flowerbeds or paths. One good idea is to set a strip of bricks into the area between the lawn and bed so they are set at the same level as the lawn. That way, when you're mowing, you can run the mower over the bricks to be sure the grass is cut right to the edge. If you water the lawn, water deeply and infrequently.

If the lawn area covers different elevations, you can avoid mowing difficulties by planting the slope with ground covers. You can also design these transition areas to include steps, perhaps combined with some trellising and new flowerbeds on either side. If you want different sections or "rooms" in your garden, make these sloping areas do double-duty by also acting as the demarcation between one part and the other. It may take a season to get the plants on the slope established as they will need extra watering in dry weather and special attention during wet weather when erosion can cause problems, but once they're established, the hard part is over. Replacing other parts of the lawn with flowerbeds or paved areas can also cut down on mowing, fertilizing, and watering chores, but don't plan too many intricate curves around flowerbeds — keep lines straight or gently curved for ease of mowing. Get rid of grass growing in places where you have to cut it by hand or with a rotary trimmer — under trees and shrubs and along fences, for example. Use mulch or ground covers in these areas.

If you're planning for a brick patio or path, it's worth hiring a professional to lay it. They can lay the foundation firmly and set the bricks tightly together so that weeds will have a hard time getting through — one time-consuming job is pulling all those weeds that seem to be able to grow in the darnedest places!

Well-trimmed hedges are beautiful, but they're high maintenance. Replace them with shrubs that don't need geometric pruning, or use fencing or trellises on which you grow vines. These will also act as windbreaks, which will protect your plants so they are not as stressed and therefore better able to resist diseases and insects. When you plant trees and shrubs, make sure they have enough room to develop as they grow, or you'll spend countless hours pruning to keep them from crowding other plants or outgrowing their space.

> If grass clippings don't create too thick a layer, leave them on the lawn after mowing -- it cuts down on maintenance, and they will add more nutrients to the soil as they decompose. Better still, use a mulching mower. I have used mine for fifteen years and have found that grass clippings do not lead to a build-up of thatch in the lawn.

When you're choosing plants, get ones that will definitely be winter hardy in your area. You might have to provide winter protection for the first year of a plant's life, but after that you want to be confident that it can make it on its own.

Check the section on Environmentally Friendly Gardening for some plants that don't need much watering — they're great for the low-maintenance garden, too. Here are some others that are undemanding — they don't need deadheading, they tolerate dry conditions, they don't need fertilizing, and they're resistant to pests and diseases.

The spreading ground covers ensure that this garden will require little in the way of maintenance.

I've included a few trees, though you can't get around the fact that deciduous trees drop their leaves, but raking leaves doesn't have to be a big chore — out of the whole gardening season, it takes only a few hours in total to rake up an average urban garden.

🌷 Astilbe (*Astilbe*): perennial

- Begonia (*Begonia*): annual

- Bergenia (*Bergenia*): perennial

- Bleeding heart (*Dicentra*): perennial

- Columbine (*Aquilegia*): perennial

- Coreopsis (*Coreopsis*): annual and perennial varieties

- Cornflower (*Centaurea cyanus*): annual

- Creeping juniper (*Juniperus horizontalis*): evergreen shrub

- Creeping phlox (*Phlox subulata*): perennial

- Daylilies (*Hemerocallis*): perennial

- Euonymus (*Euonymus*): evergreen vines

- Foamflower (*Tiarella cordifolia*): perennial

- Forsythia (*Forsythia*): deciduous shrub

- Hosta (*Hosta*): perennial

- Impatiens (*Impatiens*): annual

- Japanese barberry (*Berberis thunbergii*): deciduous shrub

- Lady's mantle (*Alchemilla*): perennial

- Lamium (*Lamium*): perennial

- Lily of the valley (*Convallaria*): perennial

- Oakleaf hydrangea (*Hydrangea quercifolia*): deciduous shrub

- Pachysandra (*Pachysandra*): perennial

- Periwinkle (*Vinca*): perennial

- Rose of Sharon (*Hibiscus syriacus*): deciduous shrub

- Sedum (*Sedum*): perennial

- Snapdragon (*Antirrhinum*): annual

- Verbena (*Verbena*): perennial; some grown as annuals

The Water Garden

Water, whether still or moving, gives a sense of peace and tranquillity to the garden. But even if there's not room for a water garden or, for reasons of child safety, you decide not to have one, you can still introduce water to the garden in a variety of ways.

A beautiful bowl sitting on the edge of a deck, on a step, or bench looks lovely. Then pour in some water — suddenly it comes to life, reflecting the blue sky or overhanging green leaves. It's a simple matter of topping up the water every day and cleaning out bits of debris that drop in. You could add a smooth black stone, slightly off centre, as a place for dragonflies to rest.

Other alternatives to the full water garden include wall fountains and pebble fountains. Wall fountains are easy to find in most garden centres and are easy to assemble — they dress up a small garden quickly. Because they're attached to the wall they don't take up much space. Hide the hardware — the tubing and pump behind the wall — and have fun designing surrounding foliage. The water will gently flow from a spout into a basin and then be recycled. The range of wall fountains is constrained only by imagination. No matter the style of your garden, you can find one to suit — from gargoyles to seashells to a simple copper lip from which the water flows in a sheet.

Pebble fountains are similar to wall fountains, except the hardware and water reservoir are hidden in the ground. A strong mesh screen is placed over them and covered by river pebbles. An unobtrusive piece of piping delivers the water, which gushes over the pebbles and back into the reservoir, where it's pumped up again. An alternative design uses a rock or millstone through which a hole has been drilled. A tube from the water reservoir is fed into the hole and it delivers the water that splashes down the sides of the rock and back into the reservoir. All these — the wall fountain, the pebble fountain, and rock or millstone fountain — make stunning focal points, especially in the small garden.

It's not a big step from these ideas to a water garden, complete with plants and fish. If you have small children, install a fence through which the water garden can be observed. Gates or removable panels give access when you need to do some upkeep. Such fences, whether constructed yourself from lattice or commissioned from a specialist working in wrought iron, have the added benefit of keeping raccoons and cats away as well.

It's nice to have the water garden near the house, where it's easily visible from windows, but there are situations in which a water garden set farther away from the house can act as a focal point, enticing the visitor down the entire length of the yard.

Water gardens can be built into the ground or incorporated in a deck. Square or rectangular water gardens, edged with paving stones or bricks, are appropriate in a formal garden. In other styles, such as a cottage or natural garden, an irregular shape is more in keeping. It's easy to get carried away and start to plan waterfalls, meandering streams, and bridges, but in most small urban lots, such busyness will detract from the effect you want to achieve. Simplicity is the key to good design.

The following plants are at home in or near water and have particularly interesting foliage.

- Arrow arum (*Peltandra virginica*): hardy; arrow-shaped, rich green shiny leaves; pea-green flowers; plant around margins of pond.

- Cattail (*Typha*): hardy; tall sword-shaped leaves and brown pokers; best in large ponds; shallow or deeper water.

- Parrot's feather (*Myriophyllum proserpinacoides*): tender; light green feathery leaves; nice at edge of pond.

- Umbrella palm (also known as paper plant) (*Cyperus*): tender — bring indoors in winter; tall stems from which issue an

Water Plants

Many water plants will survive the winter with only a little preparation. Cut back foliage of the hardy plants and move them to the deepest part of the pond. Reeds and rushes can be left standing, but their dead foliage will need to be removed early in the spring. Some tender water plants such as tropical water lilies can be wintered inside, but other plants, such as water hyacinth and water lettuce, are best treated as annuals. Goldfish and koi will survive if the water is at least 90 cm (3 feet) deep and there is an airhole in the ice. The hole can be created by a bubbler or small heater made especially for the purpose. Never attempt to make a hole in the ice by banging the ice. It will produce shock waves that kill the fish.

If you haven't the space or interest in planning a separate herb garden or if you want to carry the English cottage theme out, tuck a few herbs among your flowers. Parsley can act as more than a garnish on a plate! Plants such as chives can repel pests, as well as look attractive in the flowerbed.

explosion of starry spiky leaves; plant around margins of pond.

- Water lettuce (*Pistia stratiotes*): treat as annual; has attractive blue-green leaves; floats on pond surface.
- Water hyacinth (*Eichhornia*): treat as annual; curving leaves that arise from bulbous pods; mauve flowers; floats on pond surface.
- Water lilies (*Nymphaea*): hardy and tender types; flat, green floating leaves and pretty flowers in a range of colours from white through to deep red; place in pots in water about 30 cm (1 foot) deep.

A water feature doesn't always need plants. This scene takes its beauty from the reflection of surrounding plants and ever-changing sky.

The Herb Garden

A herb garden is within the reach of just about anyone, from a high-rise gardener to a country dweller with extensive land. Most herbs are undemanding and satisfying to grow. Their long tradition in the fields of medicine and cooking, as well as many other uses, is appealing to people who have no other interest in gardening.

You can set aside a section of the garden to grow herbs, or in a small garden devote the entire space to herbs — just be sure to choose a sunny spot. If you're going to use the herbs for cooking, a place near the kitchen or barbecue area is best. The soil should be well drained and — surprisingly, perhaps — fairly poor. Most herbs are not plants that thrive on loads of compost or manure, although added humus can improve the drainage of heavy soils. Those that will do well in normal garden soil, and need to be treated the same way as vegetables, are mint, chives, parsley, summer savoury, basil, and dill. If your soil is clay, don't give up. Design raised beds or plan to use containers instead.

An advantage of growing herbs in containers is that you can move them around to follow the sun if there's no spot in your garden that receives all-day sun. You can also grow herbs in wall baskets, hanging baskets, and window boxes, so don't confine yourself to the good old terra-cotta pot. The important thing is that the drainage should be good.

The following list includes herbs that are not only good to use in cooking but also attractive in the garden.

- Basil (*Ocimum basilicum*)
- Bay (*Laurus*)
- Chamomile (*Chamaemelum*)
- Chives (*Allium schoenoprasum*)
- Dill (*Anethum graveolens*)
- Parsley (*Petroselinum*)
- Rosemary (*Rosmarinus officinalis*)
- Sage (*Salvia officinalis*)
- Thyme (*Thymus vulgaris*)

A knot garden often springs to mind when the subject of growing herbs comes up. It makes a nice formal planting and can be as simple or complex as you desire. Knot gardens are plantings designed to make an intricate pattern and are similar to parterre, which I discussed earlier. In the spaces between the edging materials, plant selections of herbs. The edging plants are often not garden herbs themselves; some likely plants for the outline are santolina, dwarf junipers, and boxwood. However, you can also use herbs, especially those that take well to clipping, such as lavender, thyme, or bay. Use some evergreens for the outline or the interior planting so the pattern will be interesting in winter. Site the knot garden where you can view it from above so you can appreciate the design you've worked out. When you prune the edging material, don't always just snip off the ends of the plants, but take some branches from the interior of the plant to allow light and air into the centre, which will help to keep the plants healthy.

The Rock Garden

Installing a rock garden is a good solution for dealing with a sloping area, especially one that's in a sunny but protected situation. Many of the plants used in rock or alpine gardens have creeping or tumbling growth habits, so the slope allows them to follow their natural inclinations. Also, the site should drain well, so again, the slope is a good choice. However, if you're stuck with a flat site and yearn for a rock garden, some options are to build one up with imported earth and rocks, make a freestanding raised bed, or use containers to grow your alpine plants in. And if you're one of those lucky people with a rocky outcropping on your property, all you'll likely

need to do is add the plants, with perhaps some extra soil to get them started.

A rock garden is not low maintenance — weeds are an ongoing problem, so you'll need to keep a careful eye on them. However, frequent watering is not usually necessary once the plants have become established.

Plan to use rock that matches your natural surroundings. When the time comes to position them, do so with care. They should look as if they've been there for years and have every right to be there. Choose the weathered face of the rock to face out, with the largest surface of the rock uppermost. Set the rock at a slight upward angle — that is, so that water runs back into the soil rather than flowing off the edge of the rock. As much rock should be buried as exposed, which may seem like a waste of good rock. But there are several good reasons for doing this. One is that it helps to make the rock look as if it's been there, if not for eons, at

Delicate rock garden plants create mini-compositions of great beauty.

least for a reasonable length of time. Another is that the soil under the rock will be cool, providing cool conditions that the roots of the plants will seek out. Finally, if you're going to be clambering on the rocks to weed and plant, you want to feel confident that they are well secured.

When you're laying the rocks, look for the strata lines in the stones and place all stones horizontally to maintain their natural look. Unlike brick laying, do not overlap the joints, but match them up with the rock below; this will aid good drainage. In addition, don't plan the rock garden to be too high in relation to its spread. A good rule of thumb is that for every 30 cm (1 foot) in height, the garden should be 120 to 150 cm (4 to 5 feet) wide at its base.

Because many alpine plants are spring flowering, becoming dormant in the summer, introduce some dwarf perennials or low-growing annuals for colour throughout the season. It might not be a true alpine garden, but it will be interesting for longer. Many types of dwarf bulbs will add to the spring colour.

Dwarf upright shrubs and conifers look best planted at the base of the rocks. Prostrate plants, those that cascade and tumble, should be planted so that their new growth will tumble down the rock. Plants that form rosettes, such as hens and chickens, can be tucked into vertical crevices. Small stone chips make a natural-looking mulch for this type of garden.

Rock gardens can be built just about anywhere — against a wall, down a slope, or on a mound.

Before you begin the planting, consult your plans again, or sketch out the placement you have in mind to see if the various shapes and sizes of the plants are complementary. It's often tempting to try to cram a lot into a rock garden at the beginning, but some creeping plants can grow quite quickly and can take over and smother other less vigorous plants.

The following plants, not all of them true alpines, are good for beginners, but if the bug bites, join a specialty club. Many alpine gardening clubs exchange seeds of plants that may never appear in your garden centre, so it's a good way to enlarge your collection at a price you'll find agreeable.

- 🌸 Alpine poppy (*Papaver alpinum*): perennial

- 🌸 Alyssum (*Lobularia maritima*): annual

- 🌸 Aubretia (*Aubretia*): perennial

- 🌸 Creeping phlox (*Phlox subulata*): perennial

- 🌸 Creeping veronica (*Veronica alpina*): perennial

- 🌸 Saxifrage (*Saxifraga*): perennial

- 🌸 Sedum (*Sedum*): perennial

- 🌸 Thrift (*Armeria*): perennial

- 🌸 Thyme (*Thymus*): annual and perennial varieties

The Coastal Garden

Gardening by the sea has its own rewards, pleasures, and problems. Gardeners on the coasts have the same problems many of us have — winds, changing weathers, soil problems — but they face a few extra challenges. Their winds are more constant and unyielding, especially on the east coast, than the winds inland, and when they blow, they carry with them salt, frequently a plant killer.

Happily, these gardeners can thwart to some degree the effects of the sea. They should look to see which plants are surviving naturally with no problem. These are the durable plants that have adapted to the sometimes harsh environment, and they are the best ones to use to build a screen to protect your garden from the wind. Buy your plants from local nurseries and garden centres, for they will stock the local plant material.

Another challenge for seaside gardeners is to capitalize on the view, a situation that can conflict with the need to protect the plants. Situating sitting areas where they will be not too exposed but will also afford a place to appreciate the view adds to the conditions the gardener thinks about when planning the garden. However, by cleverly planting windbreaks, installing screens, and taking advantage of varying elevations, you may achieve the desired result of emphasizing the view while still having a satisfying garden.

The condition of the soil itself needs to be addressed too. Soil near the sea is often sandy and poor in nutrients. Organic matter — lots of it — will need to be dug in or used as mulch on existing plantings. Seaside soil is often acid. Seaweed, which will be in plentiful supply, is a marvellous soil conditioner.

The list below presents some plants for seaside conditions.

For Windbreaks

- 🌸 Koster blue spruce (*Picea pungens 'Koster'*): salt tolerant; Zone 2.

- 🌸 Japanese black pine (*Pinus thunbergii*): salt tolerant; Zone 5.

- 🌸 Russian olive (*Elaeagnus angustifolia*): salt tolerant; withstands winds and poor soils; Zone 2.

Shrubs

- 🌸 Bearberry (*Arctostaphylos uva-ursi*): acid soil; Zone 2.

- Mountain laurel (*Kalmia*): plant in sheltered position in acid soil; Zone 5.

- Rhododendrons (*Rhododendron*): plant in sheltered position in acid soil; various zones.

- Rugosa rose (*Rosa rugosa*): salt-tolerant, good in sandy soil; Zone 2.

For Sheltered Seaside Spots

- Beach pea (*Lathyrus littoralis*)

- California poppy (*Eschscholzia californica*)

- Thrift (*Armeria*)

- Rock cresses (*Arabis*)

- Sea holly (*Eryngium maritima*)

- Sedum (*Sedum*)

- Sun roses (*Helianthemum*)

Place scented plants close to the garden path, so you can enjoy their fragrance while you walk.

The Fragrant Garden

This garden could also be called a garden to attract butterflies and birds or a nighttime garden. It's easy to see why birds and butterflies like a fragrant garden, but you may not know that many scented flowers are light coloured and so stand out in the garden at night.

Scent is one of the most reliable triggers to bring back memories. Aromatherapy uses scent to soothe and heal our bodies and emotions. With these evocative and powerful abilities, it's easy to see why scent has a place in your garden. Tracking down scented plants is becoming more difficult, however. As hybridizers work to bring us bigger, more colourful, longer lasting, disease-, and insect-resistant blooms, scent is getting lost. Fortunately, we still have a reasonably good selection of plants from which to choose.

The best places to situate a fragrant garden or flowerbed — you don't have to give the entire garden over to scented plants — are near a window, patio or deck, or along a path. These are the places you, your family, and guests will be sitting or walking. Scent is a matter of personal taste, though, so use some restraint. A scented walkway is a great method of using different scents — along the path, intersperse the scented plants with more lightly scented ones so you can enjoy each individually. Instead of having many scented flowers blooming at the same time, choose plants that bloom in sequence. Other than these few suggestions, the design of the fragrant garden can be pretty much what you choose.

One of the side benefits of a scented garden will be the butterflies you'll attract. In addition to scent, butterflies are partial to highly coloured flowers, especially favouring wild plants. If you have the space — at least an acre — leave some of it wild.

The English cottage garden lends itself easily to incorporating fragrance, particularly with the use of roses — but again, don't assume that all roses are heavily scented.

The air in spring is often full of mock orange, though some find it rather cloying after a time, and fall air is perfumed by the sweetly scented butterfly bush, which, as its name suggests, attracts butterflies. Here are some other plants to choose from.

🌺 Artemisia (*Artemisia*): perennial

🌺 Autumn clematis (*Clematis paniculata*): perennial vine

🌺 Carnation (*Dianthus*): perennial

🌺 Common mignonette (*Reseda odorata*): annual

🌺 Freesia (*Freesia*): tender bulb

🌺 Hyacinth (*Hyacinth*): hardy bulb

🌺 Lavender (*Lavandula angustifolia*): perennial

🌺 Lilac (*Syringa*): deciduous shrub

🌺 Lily (*Lilium*): perennial

🌺 Lily of the valley (*Convallaria*): perennial

🌺 Nicotiana (*Nicotiana*): annual

🌺 Peony (*Paeonia*): perennial

🌺 Rosemary (*Rosmarinus officinalis*): perennial

🌺 Scented geranium (*Pelargonium*): annual

🌺 Stock (*Matthiola bicornis*): annual

🌺 Sweet pea (*Lathyrus odoratus*): annual

🌺 Thyme (*Thymus*): perennial — releases scent when touched

On the pages that follow, I've included sample design plans for all of the theme gardens discussed in this chapter. Use the design plans for inspiration — or follow them in detail. Whichever you choose, you will be well on your way to creating your dream garden.

The Meadow Garden

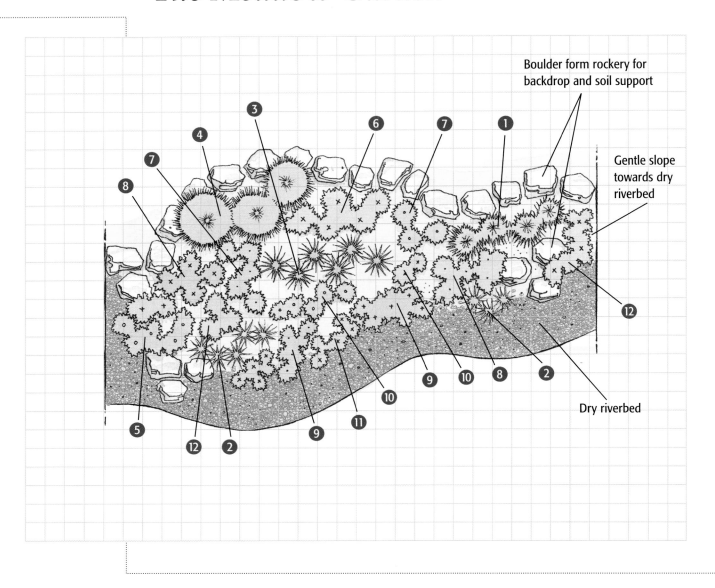

Boulder form rockery for backdrop and soil support

Gentle slope towards dry riverbed

Dry riverbed

1 Needle and thread feather grass (*Stipa capillata*)

2 Mexican feather grass (*Stipa tenuissima*)

3 Canadian wild rye grass (*Elymus canadensis*)

4 Plume grass (*Erianthus*)

5 Goldenrod (*Solidago*)

6 Beebalm (*Monarda*)

7 Coreopsis (*Coreopsis*)

8 Phlox (*Phlox paniculata*)

9 Blazing star (*Liatris*)

10 Heath aster (*Aster ericoides*)

11 Wild strawberry (*Fragaria virginiana*)

12 Queen Anne's lace (*Daucus carota*)

In a country setting, meadow gardens fit in naturally with open fields, pastures, and distant groves of trees as a backdrop. In this plan, the site is on a slight incline. The dry riverbed, formed by stones and pebbles at the front of the bed, allows for good drainage from the top of the bed to the bottom. It's a preferable solution to a ditch, which might get wet and soggy. The plants chosen will withstand drought, wind, and blazing sun. In addition to the interest provided by the sloping site, the plants themselves vary in height. The sketch shows what the plantings will look like in mid-summer.

The Shade Garden

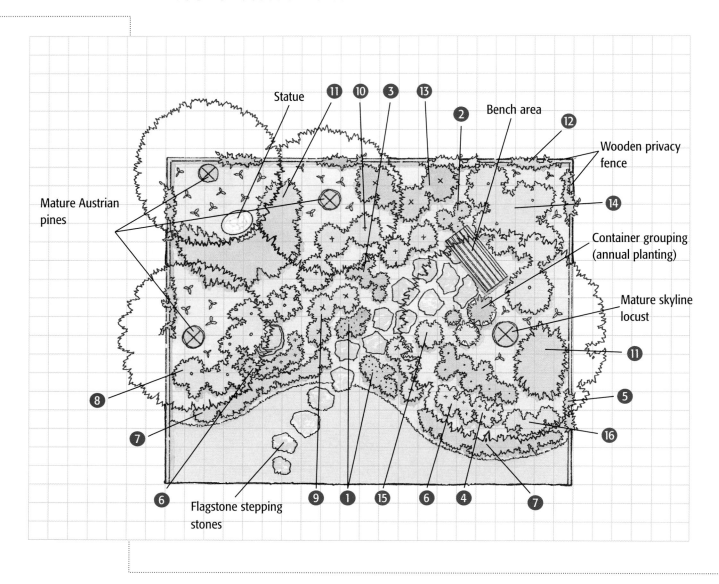

Statue

Bench area

Wooden privacy fence

Mature Austrian pines

Container grouping (annual planting)

Mature skyline locust

Flagstone stepping stones

1 Carpet campanula *(Campanula carpatica)*

2 Solomon's seal *(Polygonatum biflorum)*

3 Chinese dwarf astilbe *(Astilbe* 'Pumila'*)*

4 Foxglove *(Digitalis)*

5 Climbing hydrangea *(Hydrangea petiolaris)*

6 Begonia *(Begonia)*

7 Lamium *(Lamium* 'Pink Pewter'*)*

8 Dwarf rhododendron *(Rhododendron)*

9 Hosta *(Hosta sieboldiana* 'Elegans'*)*

10 Emerald gaiety euonymus *(Euonymus* 'Emerald gaiety'*)*

11 Yew *(Taxus cuspidata)*

12 Euonymus *(Euonymus sarcoxie)*

13 Japanese kerria *(Kerria japonica)*

14 Silverleaf dogwood *(Cornus* 'Elegantissima'*)*

15 Bleeding heart *(Dicentra spectabilis)*

16 Bergenia *(Bergenia)*

Sweet woodruff *(Galium odoratum)*

In this shady retreat, brightness is provided by the dogwood and euonymus, both of which have silver or creamy edges to their variegated leaves. The impression is of a woodland at the bottom of the garden. Note the grouping of containers at the base of the tree. The soil around tree trunks is frequently dry, difficult to dig, and, of course, in fairly deep shade. The solution? At the trunk, group containers filled with shade-loving annuals. You can control the moisture and soil to ensure healthy, productive plants. The season illustrated is the spring; in the summer, the garden will be lush and cool when other plants are blooming.

The Environmentally Friendly Garden

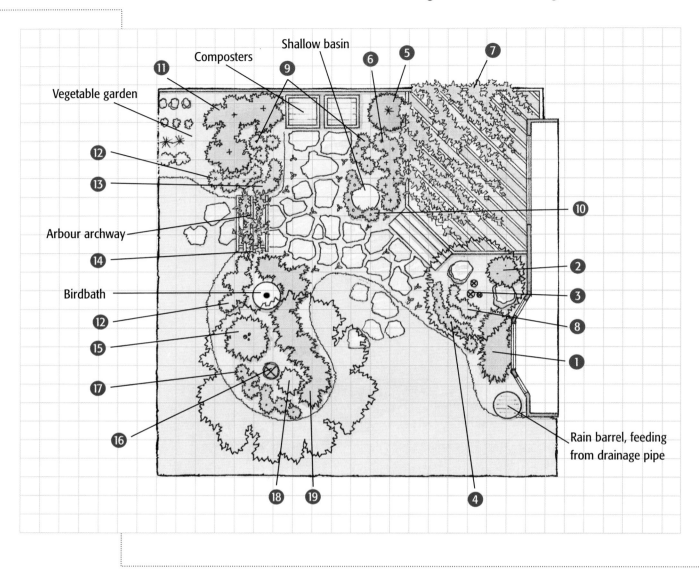

Composters

Shallow basin

Vegetable garden

Arbour archway

Birdbath

Rain barrel, feeding from drainage pipe

1. Dense spreading yew (*Taxus*)
2. Hosta (*Hosta* 'Summer Fragrance')
3. Staghorn sumac (*Rhus typhina*)
4. Thrift (*Armeria maritima*)
5. Pyramid yew (*Taxus*)
6. Purple coneflower (*Echinacea purpurea*)
7. Silver lace vine (*Polygonum aubertii*)
8. Bugleweed (*Ajuga reptans*)
9. Sedum (*Sedum spectabile*)
10. Candytuft (*Iberis umbellata*)
11. Oregon grape (*Mahonia aquifolium*)
12. Coreopsis (*Coreopsis*)
13. Carpet bellflower (*Campanula carpatica*)
14. Trumpet vine (*Campsis radicans*)
15. Lilac (*Syringa*)
16. Skyline locust (*Robinia*)
17. Blue salvia (*Salvia*)
18. Hosta (*Hosta sieboldiana* 'Elegans')
19. Cotoneaster (*Cotoneaster*)
℣ Periwinkle (*Vinca minor*)

Large areas of grass have been done away with to cut down on mowing, watering, fertilizing, and spraying with chemicals. The house is cooled naturally by the locust and the sumac, which is near the bay window. The shaded arbour provides more cooling to the house. A rain barrel collects rainwater for use in the garden. Two composters are located near the house for easy access and are also close to the vegetable garden so waste can be easily transported to the bins and finished compost, in turn, is taken back to the beds. Birds and small creatures are attracted to the shallow water basin near the arbour and another birdbath is set in a sheltered flowerbed. Birds are attracted to the berries and fruit on shrubs such as the staghorn sumac, shown in its autumn glory.

The Low-Maintenance Garden

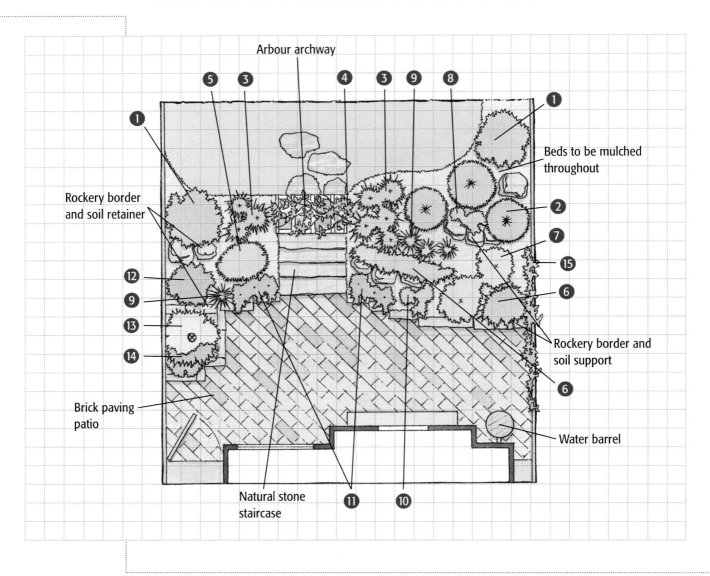

Arbour archway

Beds to be mulched throughout

Rockery border and soil retainer

Rockery border and soil support

Brick paving patio

Water barrel

Natural stone staircase

1 Rose of Sharon (*Hibiscus syriacus*)

2 Dwarf Alberta spruce (*Picea glauca conica*)

3 Daylily (*Hemerocallis*)

4 Sweet autumn clematis (*Clematis paniculata*)

5 Mugho pine (*Pinus mugo mugo*)

6 Juniper (*Juniperus horizontalis*)

7 Oakleaf hydrangea (*Hydrangea quercifolia*)

8 Snapdragon (*Antirrhinum*)

9 Blue fescue grass (*Festuca*)

10 Bergenia (*Bergenia*)

11 Creeping phlox (*Phlox subulata*)

12 Emerald gaiety euonymus (*Euonymus 'Emerald gaiety'*)

13 Caragana (*Caragana*)

14 Autumn joy sedum (*Sedum 'Autumn Joy'*)

15 Climbing hydrangea (*Hydrangea petiolaris*)

An easy-care patio is edged by a rockery with firm retaining walls to keep edging to a minimum. The shrubs and evergreens have been selected for their undemanding natures — the dwarf spruce and weeping caragana need virtually no pruning to maintain their natural shape. The plants don't produce masses of autumn leaves, either, so raking never becomes a chore. Perennials are chosen for their compact, restrained growth; in addition, they don't spread so there are no runners or roots to be cut back continually. Keep weeds to a minimum with a good mulching of bark chips. The grassed area is used for recreation, and because there are few edges and no cut-out flower beds, mowing is quick and easy.

The Water Garden

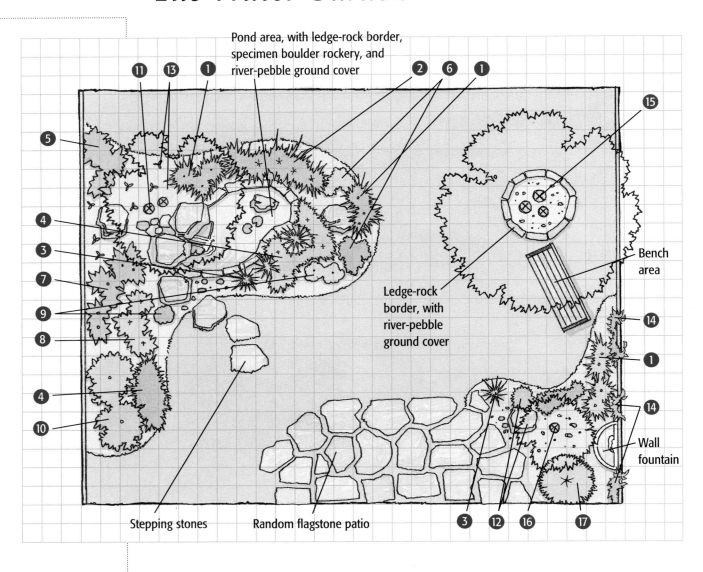

Pond area, with ledge-rock border, specimen boulder rockery, and river-pebble ground cover

Ledge-rock border, with river-pebble ground cover

Bench area

Wall fountain

Stepping stones

Random flagstone patio

1 Siberian iris (*Iris sibirica*)

2 Dwarf cattail (*Typha minima*)

3 Blue sedge (*Carex glauca*)

4 Juniper (*Juniperus horizontalis*)

5 Hosta (*Hosta sieboldiana* 'Elegans')

6 Irish moss (*Sagina subulata*)

7 Lady fern (*Athyrium filix-femina*)

8 Hosta (*Hosta* 'Ginko Craig')

9 Flowering kale (*Brassica*)

10 Azalea (*Rhododendron mucronulatum*)

11 Japanese maple (*Acer palmatum*)

12 Sedum (*Sedum spathulifolium*)

13 Water lily (*Nymphaea*)

14 Boston ivy (*Parthenocissus tricuspidata*)

15 Saucer magnolia (*Magnolia soulangiana*)

16 Weeping cutleaf Japanese maple (*Acer palmatum ornatum*)

17 Mugho pine (*Pinus mugo mugo*)

❦ Sweet woodruff (*Galium odoratum*)

It's spring and the magnolia is about to burst into bloom! These ornamental shrubs are best set apart, as done here, where their spring glory can be appreciated. From the bench, you can have a different perspective as you look back at the patio and house. In the spring and through the rest of the gardening season, though, the big attraction will be the water. The pond is surrounded by ornamental grasses and Siberian iris; the Japanese maple hangs over the pond and rocks. The stepping stones make the pond accessible — sit on the rocks and dangle your toes in the water or watch the fish gliding among the water plants. The wall fountain continues the theme of water, adds character, and gives the soothing sound of splashing water.

The Herb Garden

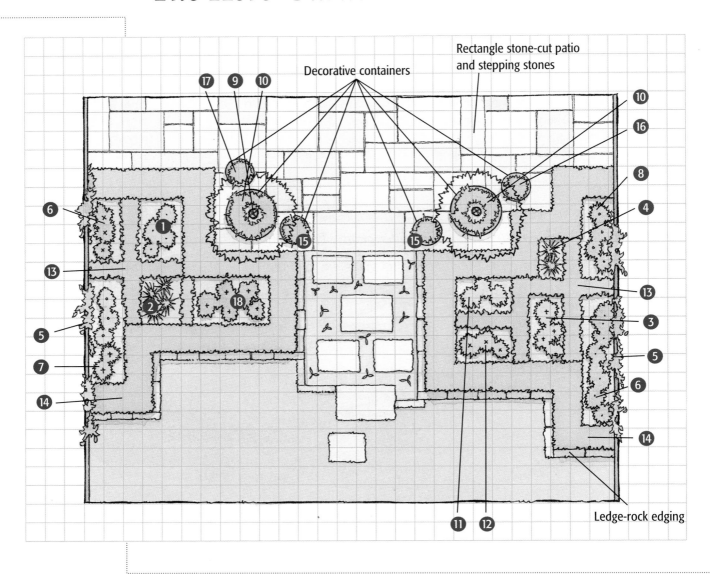

Decorative containers

Rectangle stone-cut patio and stepping stones

Ledge-rock edging

1 Basil (*Ocimum basilicum*)

2 Chives (*Allium schoenoprasum*)

3 Rubin basil (*Ocimum basilicum* 'Rubin')

4 Garlic chives (*Allium tuberosum*)

5 Bittersweet vine (*Solanum dulcamara*)

6 German chamomile (*Matricaria recutita*)

7 Fennel (*Foeniculum*)

8 Dill (*Anethum graveolens*)

9 Camphor (*Cinnamom camphora*)

10 Geranium (*Pelargonium hortorum*)

11 Rosemary (*Rosmarinus officinalis*)

12 Oregano (*Origanum*)

13 Lavender (*Lavandula angustifolia*)

14 Boxwood (*Buxus* 'Green velvet')

15 Parsley (*Petroselinum*)

16 Sage (*Salvia officinalis*)

17 Mint (*Mentha*)

18 Tarragon (*Artemisia*)

Thyme (*Thymus*)

Herbs love heat, so this is a garden at its prime at the height of summer. The design is formal — squared-off clipped boxwood hedges, symmetrical layout, rectangular paving stones, and the wrought iron railings. Inside the hedge, which defines the shape and contains it, are further "hedges" of lavender, which provides colour, texture, and scent, lightening the effect of the dense boxwood. Herbs have been chosen for their flowers and foliage in addition to their medicinal or culinary usefulness. Containers are planted with parsley, mint, and sage. The large urns hold camphor trees, which are treated as annuals in our climate. Fragrant creeping herbs such as one of the many thymes can be planted between paving stones to release their sweet scent as you walk on them.

The Rock Garden

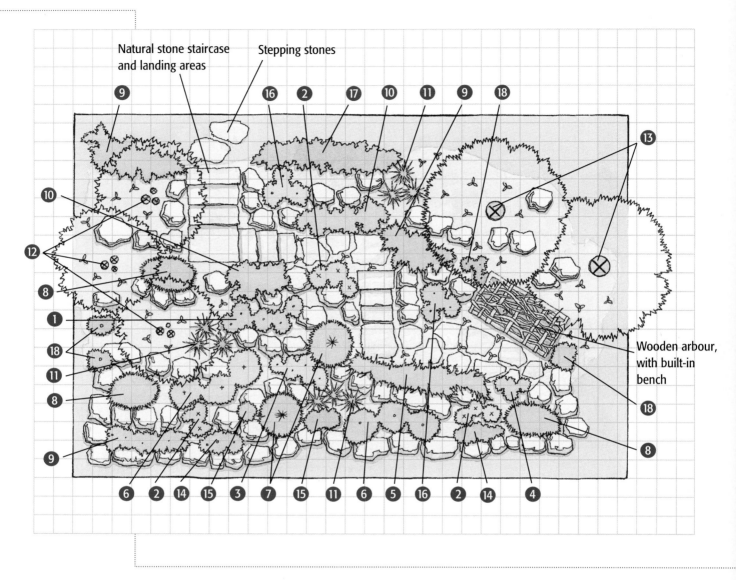

Natural stone staircase and landing areas

Stepping stones

Wooden arbour, with built-in bench

1. Alpine poppy (*Papaver alpinum*)
2. Autumn joy sedum (*Sedum* 'Autumn Joy')
3. Saxifrage (*Saxifraga*)
4. Thrift (*Armeria maritima*)
5. Juniper (*Juniperus horizontalis*)
6. Spirea (*Spiraea bumalda* 'Gold Mound')
7. Dwarf Alberta spruce (*Picea glauca conica*)
8. Mugho pine (*Pinus mugo mugo*)
9. Rockspray cotoneaster (*Cotoneaster horizontalis*)
10. Creeping phlox (*Phlox subulata*)
11. Variegated dwarf sedge (*Carex conica*)
12. Staghorn sumac (*Rhus typhina*)
13. Austrian pine (*Pinus nigra*)
14. Rock cress (*Aubrieta*)
15. Ice plant (*Delosperma*)
16. Cranesbill (*Geranium*)
17. Rockrose (*Helianthemum*)
18. Edelweiss (*Leontopodium alpinum*)

Creeping thyme (*Thymus*) (inbetween stepping stones)

Broom (*Genista*) (on open sloped areas)

Designed for a site that slopes into a ravine, this plan uses plants that withstand drought. The sunny dry area is planted with sumac and pine, whose shallow roots help prevent erosion. A stone path, a focal point from farther back in the garden, leads to this lovely little hideaway, taking you right to the pretty twig seat. The slabs of natural stone provide good footing and make it easy to carry out the light maintenance needed. The dwarf nursery stock keeps maintenance low as it keeps its shape well and needs little pruning. Shade- and drought-tolerant plants grow under the trees, and sun lovers are elsewhere. Planted among the paving stones near the bench is thyme; the scent is released as you walk on the plants.

The Coastal Garden

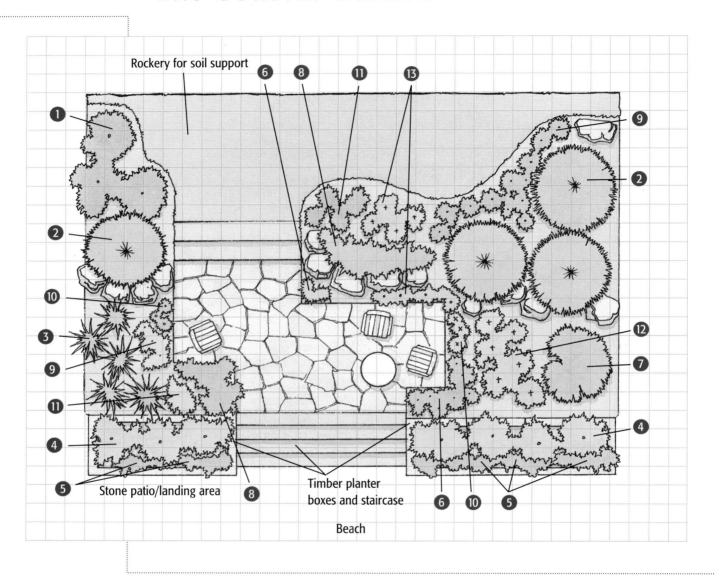

Rockery for soil support

Stone patio/landing area

Timber planter boxes and staircase

Beach

1. Mountain laurel (*Kalmia latifolia*)
2. Japanese black pine (*Pinus thunbergii*)
3. Cattail (*Typha*)
4. Rugosa rose (*Rosa rugosa*)
5. Variegated Russian sedum (*Sedum kamtschaticum variegatum*)
6. Thrift (*Armeria maritima*)
7. Bearberry (*Arctostaphylos uva-ursi*)
8. Sun rose (*Helianthemum*)
9. California poppy (*Eschscholzia californica*)
10. Creeping lily turf (*Liriope spicata*)
11. Variegated sedum (*Sedum alboroseum*)
12. Cranberry (*Vaccinium vitis-idaea*)
13. Geranium (*Pelargonium hortorum*)

Planned for the seaside, you could adapt this for any waterside garden. The aim is to provide protection in the sitting area but not to cut off the view from the house to the ocean or body of water. The plantings will withstand the elements: the harsh wind that blows in from the open water, the salt carried in from the sea, and a sandy soil. Pines have been chosen for their salt tolerance and other plants have the advantage of being low maintenance and having little need of fertilizers or organic material in the soil. The cattail grass could do with more moisture than most of the other plants, so you can either make a boggy area for them or plant them close to the water's edge of a lake, river, or pond.

The Fragrant Garden

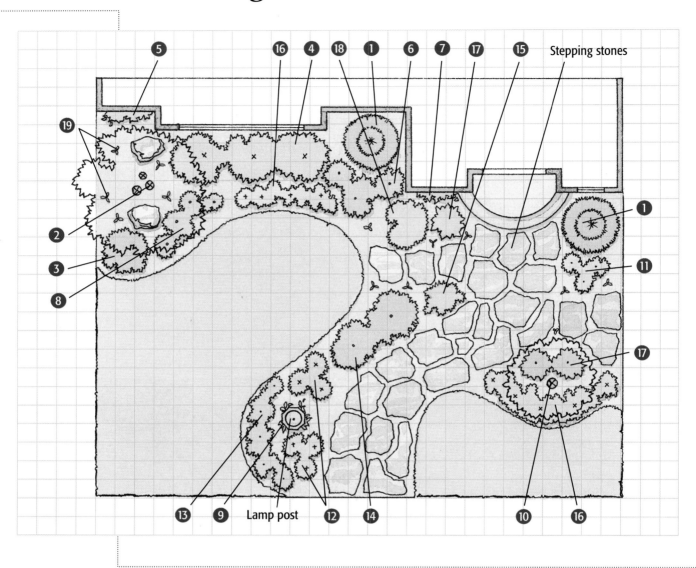

Stepping stones

Lamp post

1. Emerald cedar (*Thuja occidentalis*)
2. Serviceberry (*Amelanchier canadensis*)
3. Slender deutzia (*Deutzia gracilis*)
4. Mock orange (*Philadelphus coronarius*)
5. Euonymus (*Euonymus fortunei*)
6. Peony (*Paeonia*)
7. Climbing rose (*Rosa america*)
8. Carnations (*Dianthus*)
9. Autumn clematis (*Clematis paniculata*)
10. Fragrant viburnum (*Viburnum farreri*)
11. Stock (*Matthiola bicornis*)
12. Nicotiana (*Nicotiana sylvestris*)
13. Lavender (*Lavandula angustifolia*)
14. Dwarf Korean lilac (*Syringa velutina*)
15. Rosemary (*Rosmarinus officinalis*)
16. Maiden pinks (*Dianthus deltoides* 'Maiden Pink')
17. Hosta (*Hosta sieboldiana*)
18. Emerald gaiety euonymus (*Euonymus* 'Emerald gaiety')
19. Lily of the valley (*Convallaria majalis*)
    Thyme (*Thymus*)

This garden is planned for continuous scents from spring to fall. The chosen plants will not be overpowering. Pictured here, the lilac, mock orange, lily of the valley, and fragrant viburnum fill the spring air with refreshing sweet scents. In summer, roses at the front door will do their part and pinks, nicotiana, stock, carnations, and lavender will delight passersby and visitors for most of the season. In autumn, the vigorous autumn clematis will add its perfume. The stone path meanders from the drive and the front door, easily leading your steps to the scented plants, no matter the season.

Bibliography

Adams, George. *Birdscaping Your Garden: A Practical Guide to Backyard Birds and the Plants That Attract Them.* Emmaus, Pennsylvania: Rodale Press, 1994.

Bennett, Jennifer, ed. *The Harrowsmith Landscaping Handbook.* Camden East: Camden House, 1985.

Boisset, Caroline, and Fayal Greene. *The Garden Sourcebook: A Practical Guide to Planning and Planting.* New York: Crown Publishers, Inc., 1993.

Brookes, John. *The Book of Garden Design.* New York: Macmillan, 1991.

Brookes, John. *The Small Garden.* London: Tiger Books International, 1996.

Canadian Gardening's Creating a Garden. Toronto: Penguin Books Canada Ltd., 1996.

Canadian Gardening's Small Space Gardens. Toronto: Penguin Books Canada Ltd., 1997.

Cole, Brenda, ed. *Shade Gardens.* Camden East: Camden House, 1993.

Cole, Trevor. *The Ontario Gardener.* Vancouver/Toronto: Whitecap Books, 1991.

Cowley, Jill. *Beds and Borders for Year Round Colour.* London: Ward Lock, 1995.

Cullen, Mark. *A Greener Thumb: The Complete Guide to Gardening in Canada.* Toronto: Penguin Books, 1990.

Dale, John, and Kevin Gunnell. *The Gardener's Palette: The Complete Guide to Selecting Plants by Color.* New York: Harmony Books, 1992.

Dirr, Michael. *All About Evergreens.* San Ramon, California: Ortho Books, 1984.

Ellefson, Connie, Tom Stephens, and Doug Welsh. *Xeriscape Gardening.* New York: Macmillan Publishing Company, 1992.

Fawcett, Brian. *The Compact Garden.* Camden East: Camden House, 1992.

Ferguson, Nicola. *Right Plant, Right Place: The Indispensable Guide to the Successful Garden.* London: Macmillan, 1995.

Harper, Peter. *The Natural Garden Book.* New York: Simon & Schuster Inc., 1994.

Harris, Marjorie. *The Canadian Gardener: A Guide to Gardening in Canada.* Toronto: Random House, 1990.

Harris, Marjorie. *The Canadian Gardener's Guide to Foliage and Garden Design.* Toronto: Random House, 1993.

Harris, Marjorie. *Pocket Gardening: A Guide to Gardening in Impossible Places.* Toronto: HarperCollins, 1998.

How to Design and Build Children's Play Equipment. San Ramon, California: Ortho Books, 1986.

Johnson, Lorraine. *The Ontario Naturalized Garden: The Complete Guide to Using Native Plants.* Vancouver/Toronto: Whitecap Books, 1995.

Johnson, Lorraine. *Grow Wild!: Native Plant Gardening in Canada.* Toronto: Random House, 1998.

Lacy, Allen. *The Garden in Autumn.* New York: The Atlantic Monthly Press, 1990.

Larousse Gardening and Gardens. New York: Facts on File, 1990.

Lawson, Andrew. *The Gardener's Book of Color.* New York/Montreal: Reader's Digest Association, Inc., 1996.

Macoboy, Stirling. *The Ultimate Rose Book.* New York: Henry N. Abrams, Inc., 1993.

Marston, Ted, ed. *Annuals.* New York: Hearst Books, 1993.

Osborne, Robert. *Roses for Canadian Gardens.* Toronto: Key Porter, 1991.

Paterson, Allen. *Designing a Garden.* Camden East: Camden House, 1992.

Phillips, Ellen, and C. Colston Burrell. *Rodale's Illustrated Encyclopedia of Perennials.* Emmaus, Pennsylvania: Rodale Press, 1993.

Reader's Digest Illustrated Guide to Gardening in Canada. Montreal: The Reader's Digest Association (Canada) Ltd., 1979.

Rodale's Illustrated Encyclopedia of Gardening and Landscaping Techniques. Emmaus, Pennsylvania: Rodale Press, 1990.

Rodale's Successful Organic Gardening Low-Maintenance Landscaping. Emmaus, Pennsylvania: Rodale Press, 1994.

Shields, Dinah, and Edwinna von Baeyer. *The Reluctant Gardener: A Beginner's Guide to Gardening in Canada.* Toronto: Random House, 1992.

Stevens, Elaine, Dagmar Hungerford, Doris Fancourt-Smith, Jane Mitchell, and Ann Buffam. *The Twelve Month Gardener: A West Coast Guide.* Vancouver: Whitecap Books, 1991.

Taylor's Guide to Garden Design. Boston: Houghton Mifflin Company, 1961.

Vick, Roger. *Gardening on the Prairies.* Saskatoon: Western Producer Prairie Books, 1987.

Wilson, Lois. *Chatelaine's Gardening Book: The Complete All-Canada Guide to Garden Success.* Toronto: Maclean-Hunter Limited/Doubleday Canada Limited, 1970.

Winterrowd, Wayne. *Annuals for Connoisseurs.* Prentice Hall: New York, 1992.

Index

Contributing Editor: Wendy Thomas

Editorial Co-ordinator: Lorraine Johnson

Photography: Greg Holman

Art Direction and Design: Pronk&Associates/Joe Lepiano

Illustrations: Jack McMaster

Horticultural Editor and Garden Plans: Wendy Boyle

Copy Editor: Alison Reid

Jacket Design: Pronk&Associates

Produced for Penguin by Pronk&Associates

....

OTHER PHOTOS:

pp. 16–17: David Michael Allen; pp. 26–27: Joe Lepiano;
p. 79 Top row centre and right, bottom row: Courtesy of Unilock.

SPECIAL THANKS TO:

Jeff Scott

David Allen   Heather Mallick
Mike Assaly   Susan Manning
Karen & Michael Barbeau   Sheila McCracken
Flavio Belli   Velda Mizzi
Linda Boorman   Gerald Moldenhauer
Wendy Boyle   Keven Oheil
Sandy & Rob Chappel   Linda Pethrick
Ruth & John Crow   Charles Sammut
Rowena Dahiroc   Alison & Allen Schwartz
Juliet Del-Junco & Peggy Sampson   Jennifer & Christina Spagnolo
Telford Fenton   Karen & David Spagnolo
Estel Friedman   Ray Yohannis-Smit
Joy & David Garrick   Doug Stewart
Tim & Tina Haanstra   Penny Turner
Ann Holman   Jacob Verkade
Mary Janyan & Tom Kierans   Damaris Walker
Sue & Orn Krivel   Pam William
Monica Kuhn